COOKING FOR HENRY

The memories and recipes of Chef Jan Willemse,
former pastry chef at Dearborn Inn and
personal party chef for Henry Ford.

Chef J.A.M. Willemse

and

Eleanor Eaton

COOKING FOR HENRY

The memories and recipes of Chef Jan Willemse,
former pastry chef at Dearborn Inn and
personal party chef for Henry Ford.

by Jan Willemse
and Eleanor Eaton

THE
DONNING COMPANY
PUBLISHERS

> To my late wife, Annie

(Photo previous page and dust jacket) Fair Lane, the last home of Henry and Clara Ford, was completed in 1915 on the banks of the Rouge River in Dearborn, Michigan. Of Scottish baronial style, it was constructed of Indiana limestone. The mansion has fifty-six rooms and is located on 1,346 acres. After Mrs. Ford's death, the Henry Ford Estate–Fair Lane was given to the University of Michigan-Dearborn by the Ford Motor Company. Photograph courtesy of Jan Willemse. Hand colored on dust jacket by Eliza Midgett.

Copyright © 1993 by Jan Willemse and Eleanor V. Eaton
All rights reserved, including the right to reproduce this work in any form whatsoever without permission in writing from the publisher, except for brief passages in connection with a review. For information, write:

The Donning Company/Publishers
184 Business Park Drive, Suite 106
Virginia Beach, VA 23462

Steve Mull, General Manager
Mary Jo Kurten, Editor
Mary Eliza Midgett, Designer
Debra Y. Quesnel, Project Director
Tracey Emmons-Schneider, Project Research Coordinator
Elizabeth B. Bobbitt, Production Editor

Library of Congress Cataloging in Publication Data:
Willemse, Jan, 1900–
        Cooking for Henry : the memories and recipes of Chef Jan Willemse, former pastry chef at Dearborn Inn and personal party chef for Henry Ford I / by Chef Willemse and Eleanor Eaton.
        p. cm.
        Includes index.
        ISBN 0-89865-880-2 (alk. paper)
        1. Cookery. 2. Cookery (Soybeans) 3. Ford, Henry, 1863–1947.
    4. Dearborn (Mich.)—Description and travel. I. Eaton, Eleanor. II. Title.
    TX714.W523 1993   93-29731
        641.5—dc20   CIP
Printed in the United States of America

The elegant Early
American dining
room at the Dearborn
Inn afforded gracious
dining. Photograph
courtesy of the
Dearborn Inn

CONTENTS

Annie and I posed for this picture following our wedding March 17, 1923, in Boston, Massachusetts. We met and married only four years after I came to America from Holland. Photograph courtesy of Jan Willemse

FOREWORD

We, Jan's three sons—Gerrit, Neil, and John—consider ourselves fortunate to have a dad who cooked for Henry Ford I. This relationship enabled us to share a small part of Ford history. Because of it, we attended the Greenfield Village schools, sang on radio in the Ford chorus, and had an occasional opportunity to see and talk with the great industrialist.

The qualities our father and we admired most in Henry Ford were his simple manner, his genuine interest in his employees, their families, and his many kindnesses to them.

Dad met Eleanor Eaton, the co-author of this book, at the Ford Fair Lane home in 1988. He was attending a fund-raising luncheon for the restoration of the estate sponsored by the Women of Fair Lane. Dad had baked and brought some of Mr. Ford's favorite soybean cookies to share that afternoon.

Mrs. Eaton was writing for a local paper in Dearborn at the time and proceeded to do a feature story about Dad and his association with Mr. Ford. Through the years that followed, the two kept in touch.

Years after he retired from Ford's employ, Dad worked as executive chef for Miesel/Sysco Corporation. While at Miesel's he compiled a simple recipe pamphlet that he enjoyed giving to Miesel salesmen and customers.

Associates kept urging Dad to write a cookbook of his commercial recipes, but a scaled-down version with fewer servings. He discussed this idea with Mrs. Eaton, and they decided to collaborate on the book and include some of Dad's personal story along with it.

Dad selected and adapted his recipes while Mrs. Eaton edited, wrote the biographical text, and selected the accompanying photos. The book was published in 1993, just after Dad's ninety-third birthday. We are proud of the book—and the man who authored it. It is in some ways a reflection of a life—a sharing of simple, plain, and honest tastes. It is Dad and how he would like to be remembered.

—Gerrit, Neil, and John Willemse

Here I am (at the left) working as pastry chef in the
kitchen of the Dearborn Inn in 1933. The other men
are unidentified. Photograph courtesy of Jan Willemse

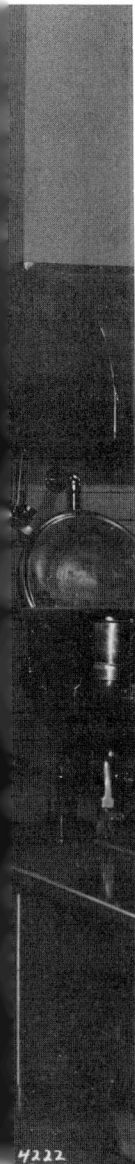

PART I
I'm Discovered by Edsel Ford

I am often asked how I happened to come to Dearborn to cook for Henry Ford. How did a young apprentice chef from Holland become pastry chef at the Dearborn Inn and the personal party chef for the famous automaker, people want to know. Some would call it luck. I say it was meant to be.

In my teens I worked as an apprentice chef for my uncle who was in the catering business in Holland. A friend had gone to America to seek his fortune, and he sent me letters telling of his success. He was making the fabulous sum of forty dollars a week.

In 1919 when I became nineteen years old, I decided that I, too, would go to this wonderful country and join my friend who was living in Boston, Massachusetts.

I worked my way across the ocean as a cook aboard a freighter, and after several delays, arrived in Boston. What was against me in looking for a job was my English. I couldn't speak the language. But I was a good cook, and I wasn't afraid of hard work. That's why Mr. Richard Brock, manager of the Brookline Hotel, hired me as second cook. Mr. Brock and I got along very well.

For relaxation my friend and I went to dances that were arranged for Belgian and Dutch immigrants. There I met Catherine Keysper. She had a sister Annie living in Canada, who she thought might like a young Dutchman. She got us to meet and after a courtship of several years, we were married in 1923.

Besides the Boston hotel, Mr. Brock also managed hotels in Maine and Florida. After I worked for him awhile he would take me with him to Maine in the summer and Florida in the winter. My wife, Annie, and our first born son, Gerrit, and I would pack up our Ford touring car and drive there.

Between seasons I'd work at L. G. Treadway's Inn in Williamston, Massachusetts. I'd help train managers—show them how to make menus, what to serve and such. Treadway had a number of Inns around the country for people of wealth.

It was in 1931 while I was cooking at the Nautilus Hotel in Miami Beach, Florida, that I met Edsel Ford. His yacht was moored in the marina, and I brought food to the crew. I didn't know who this quiet gentleman was, but I liked him. He thought I was a good cook.

Well, Edsel's father happened to be Henry Ford, the automaker. He had just opened the Dearborn Inn in Dearborn, Michigan, and Edsel thought I would be a good executive chef for the new hotel. He told his father about me, and Mr. Henry Ford wrote to me asking if I'd come to Dearborn and take the job of head chef.

But my friend Mr. Brock talked me out of it. He told me that Dearborn was just a small town far away from the rest of the world; not at all like Boston or Miami. And it was small at the time. So I turned down the offer and forgot about it. But as I said—it was meant to be that I go to Dearborn.

A couple of years later when I was in Boston I went to see a fish merchant who had connections with inns around the country. I wanted to know what was new on the market—gossip, I guess you'd call it.

"Hey, Jan," he said, "there's a fellow looking for you. Do you know John Packard? He's the manager of that new inn in Dearborn, Michigan."

I said, "Sure, he was trained at the Treadway Inn when I was there."

"Well, Treadway's running the Dearborn Inn," said the fish merchant. "I'm going to call Packard about an order. Will you talk to him?"

I said "OK," so when I got Packard on the line he asked me to come to the Dearborn Inn and be the pastry chef. He told me that by this time they'd hired Paul LeVegue as executive chef. "I'm the second manager," Packard said. "Charles Graham opened the Inn in 1931."

He asked me to try the job for three months. He was sure I'd like it and stay on. I told him I didn't know. Annie was expecting our second child, but I'd think about it. After Neil's birth I decided to give the job a try. I left my family in Boston with my in-laws and took the train to Dearborn.

Mr. Packard had arranged for everything. He gave me a nice room in Pilots' Row. That was a section in the south wing of the inn that was kept for the pilots and stewardesses from the airport that Mr. Ford had built across the road from the inn.

I liked the Dearborn Inn from the start, even though it was not up to the things that I knew. The kitchen was not as modern as those I had worked in. There was no steam for the ovens. But, its look reminded me of Boston. Even the signs were New England.

After I decided to stay on as pastry chef I went to Boston for my wife and the boys and brought them to a house I had rented in Dearborn. Annie was happy that we were settling down in one place year around for the boys' sake. Then I gave my family a tour of the inn. They thought it was beautiful. They admired its Georgian style architecture with a three-story wing on either side. The architect was Albert Kahn, I told them.

From a window in the main dining room I showed my family where the airport was across the road. The dining room was very elegant. But there was a casual coffee shop paneled in knotty pine also in the hotel. Both restaurants were served from a kitchen with stainless steel appointments made on special order for Mr. Ford.

Annie and the boys tried out the comfortable furniture in the lounge and lobby, which were in Early American style, and then inspected the bedrooms that were furnished with copies of genuine old pieces.

I told them Mr. Ford had built the inn for travelers coming in at the airport and visitors to the Edison Institute Museum and Greenfield Village. He founded the Edison Institute in 1919 as a living history exhibit.

I soon learned that the inn was also used as a club for executives and other important Dearborn citizens who met there regularly for lunch.

After a couple of weeks as pastry chef, I had my first contact with Mr. Ford. A messenger told me that the old gentleman wanted me to bake Kaiser rolls for a special event at his home, Fair Lane.

I said, "Tell Mr. Ford the flour is too soft. I need Minnesota flour for Kaiser rolls, and besides I have to have steam for the oven."

Then Ford's head miller, Mr. Schelkelton, came to see me. "Are you the wise guy who thinks Mr. Ford's flour is no good?" he asked.

I told him the Lord himself couldn't make French bread out of this flour and without steam. Well, I got what I wanted by the next day.

It wasn't long before I learned Mr. Ford didn't want any alcohol served at the inn. He was very firm about that. But, patrons sometimes asked for it, and since Treadway had a liquor license, we'd serve them. There was a movable bar in the kitchen that we would quickly cover up when we knew the boss was coming. Mr. Ford was very much against smoking, too. Well, I liked a cigarette now and then. But I'd go outside the building to smoke it.

I didn't meet the Fords personally until I had been at the inn several months. When I did, I liked them both very much. I was young and of average height. I thought Mr. Ford must be at least six feet tall. He wasn't. But he was slender and that made him seem taller than he was. He wore well tailored but plain suits.

Mrs. Ford was the picture of my mother, though she was a little heavier.

After I became better acquainted with them I found that they were both strict but fair. Mr. Ford didn't mince words. He'd come right out and say what he thought.

I met Dr. Edsel Ruddiman, Mr. Ford's food chemist, about the same time. Dr. Ruddiman and Mr. Ford had been friends since school days. The Fords thought so highly of him that they named their only son after him.

Mr. Ford was good to me and my family. With the birth of John, Annie and I now had three sons. Mr. Ford sent them all to the Greenfield Village Schools and also paid Gerry and Neal to sing in the Ford Sunday Evening Hour radio program. Johnny was still too young for that.

The Fords loved to dance, and they were very good at it. They invited my family to the Early American dances they held every week in the Lovett Hall ballroom in Greenfield Village.

The ballroom was named after Benjamin Lovett, the Fords' personal dancing master. I was asked to provide refreshments for these dances—things like finger sandwiches, punch, and cocoa. I also served coffee, but it was not very popular.

Clara Ford invited their friends from Grosse Pointe one week and Dearborn friends the next. She also often entertained her lady friends at Fair Lane mansion. These were fancy affairs with fresh flowers from her gardens on the tables.

Dr. Ruddiman's wife, Jennie, who attended the luncheons told her husband what Mrs. Ford liked, and he would tell me. So I'd make the same kind of refreshments for the dances.

I never went to the mansion to cook while the Fords lived there. They had a Finnish cook named Maria Luukonen. Sometimes Mrs. Ford's chauffeur, John Williams, a black man, helped with the cooking.

However, I would send over special breads and pastries to Fair Lane that I baked in the kitchen of the Dearborn Inn, and later in the kitchen of a building across from Dr. Ruddiman's Research Laboratory in the village. The building was used to repair antique cars that would go into the Henry Ford Museum. There was a restaurant at one end for village employees.

I also prepared the Fords' favorite pastries and breads when they were at one of their other homes in Georgia, Florida, or northern Michigan. I'd have the baked goods ready to go every time the mail was delivered to the Fords by car.

B R E A D S   A N D   P A S T R I E S

Home Style White Bread

2 tsp. dry yeast
4 c. lukewarm milk
6 Tbs. sugar
4 tsp. vegetable shortening
3 Tbs. salt
12 c. bread flour

Preheat oven to 375 degrees.
Dissolve yeast in warm milk. Mix sugar, vegetable shortening, and salt together. Add the milk and yeast mix and stir a little. Add the flour and mix to a medium firm dough. Cover the dough and let rise until it doubles in size. Punch down and let it rise again. Then place the dough on the work table and mold it into the shape you want. Place it into two, clean, greased bread pans and let it rise into a little more than double in size. Bake 30 to 35 minutes, until a nice golden color.
Yields 2 9- by 5-inch loaves

Whole Wheat Rolls or Bread

1 oz. yeast
1/2 c. lukewarm water
1/4 c. sugar
1 Tbs. salt
3 Tbs. vegetable shortening
1 Tbs. molasses
3 well beaten eggs
1 c. warm milk
3 c. bread flour
3 c. whole wheat flour

Preheat oven to 375 degrees.
Dissolve the yeast in the lukewarm water. Mix sugar, salt, vegetable shortening, and molasses. Add the beaten eggs and milk. Add the dissolved yeast and mix a little. Add the bread flour and whole wheat flour. Mix by machine with dough hook or by hand. Mix for 5 minutes until smooth. Place dough in a greased bowl, cover and let rise in a warm place until double in size. Then punch it down. Wait 20 to 30 minutes and put dough on the work table and mold into different shapes or loaves. For instance, three small buns in a muffin tin, or regular round rolls, or any shape you like. Brush each with some melted vegetable shortening. Let rise to double in size and bake for about 20 minutes.
Yields 2 dozen rolls or 2 9- by 5-inch loaves of bread

Graham Bread or Rolls

4 c. lukewarm milk
2 Tbs. dry yeast
3 level Tbs. salt
1/2 c. molasses
6 c. graham flour
7 c. bread flour
1 Tbs. vegetable shortening

Preheat oven to 375 degrees.
Dissolve yeast in warm milk. Mix salt and molasses in mixing bowl. Add the milk and yeast, mix in the graham and bread flours. Work into a smooth dough, cover with a clean towel, and let rise until double the size. Push it down, wait about 20 minutes, then form into loaves. Place them in greased bread pans or make small rolls any shape you want. Let it rise into a little more than double in size in a warm spot away from the draft. Bake 30 to 35 minutes until golden brown. When bread or rolls come out of the oven, brush with a little melted vegetable shortening or butter to keep them soft.
Yields 3 9- by 5-inch loaves or 4 dozen rolls

Raisin Bread or Hot Cross Buns

2 tsp. dry yeast
4 c. lukewarm milk
1 c. sugar
2/3 c. margarine
1 tsp. nutmeg
1 Tbs. vanilla
5 eggs
4 c. milk
12 c. all purpose flour
4 c. clean raisins (or currants)
1 1/2 c. citron chopped fine

Preheat oven to 375 degrees.
Dissolve yeast in warm milk. Mix sugar, margarine, and nutmeg for 2 minutes. Add vanilla and eggs. Then add the milk and yeast and stir a little. Add the flour, raisins (or currants) and citron. Place in a greased container. Cover it and let rise in a warm spot for 1 to 2 hours. Punch dough down after 25 to 30 minutes and shape dough into bread or hot cross buns. Let dough rise (double in size) and bake for about 15 minutes. Brush with a little butter or make a white frosting cross on top of the buns.
Yields 2 9- by 5-inch loaves of bread (or 4 dozen hot cross buns)

Plain Rolls
(Dough is good for finger rolls, Parker House, or split rolls)

4 c. lukewarm milk
3 tsp. dry yeast
2/3 c. sugar
1 c. vegetable shortening
2 Tbs. salt
3 eggs
11 heaping c. bread flour

Preheat oven to 375 degrees.
Dissolve yeast in warm milk. Mix sugar, vegetable shortening, salt, and eggs together. Add the milk and yeast mix and stir a little. Add the flour and mix to a medium firm dough. Place in a greased bowl. Cover the dough and let rise in a warm spot until it doubles in size. Punch down and let it rise for 20 to 30 minutes. Then place the dough on the work table and mold it into the roll shapes you want. Place into slightly greased pans or muffin tins. Place rolls in proofing box or warm place out of the draft until double in size. Bake 20 minutes in a brisk oven. When done, while still warm, brush them over with melted vegetable shortening if you want to have a soft roll.
Yields about 3 to 4 dozen rolls

Soft Roll Mix

1/2 c. sugar
2 Tbs. salt
1/3 c. vegetable shortening
2 eggs
2 c. warm milk
2 tsp. dry yeast
6 1/2 c. bread flour

Preheat oven to 375 degrees.
Mix sugar, salt, vegetable shortening and eggs for 2 minutes. Add the warm milk. Mix dry yeast with the flour. Mix everything together for about 5 minutes. Grease mixing bowl and let dough proof rise for 30 to 45 minutes in a warm place, covered. Punch down and let it rise again for another 30 minutes. Then place the dough on the work table and mold it into the roll shapes (split, Parker House, finger, etc.) Place rolls in proofing box or warm place out of the draft until double in size. Bake for 15 to 18 minutes until rolls are golden brown. For a soft roll, while still warm, brush them over with melted vegetable shortening.
Yields about 3 dozen rolls

Bishop Bread

Bread
1 c. vegetable shortening
1 1/2 c. brown sugar
2 tsp. salt
1 tsp. vanilla
3 eggs
2 c. milk
5 c. bread flour
2 Tbs. baking powder

Topping
1/2 c. sugar
1/3 c. vegetable shortening
3/4 c. flour
1 Tbs. cinnamon
1 tsp. salt

Preheat oven to 350 degrees.
Cream together vegetable shortening, brown sugar, and salt for about 2 minutes. Add the vanilla and eggs slowly and mix for 2 minutes more. Scrape the bowl. Add the milk. Blend in the flour and baking powder, mix altogether for 2 minutes, until smooth. Pour mixture into a well-greased and floured cake pan (12 by 18 inches). Now mix your topping (by hand is best). Place sugar, vegetable shortening, flour, cinnamon, and salt altogether in a bowl. Rub it all together for a couple of minutes until it looks like lumpy brown sugar, and put this on top of your cake mix evenly. Bake for 15 to 20 minutes until done. Cut into small squares for serving.
Yields 12 portions

Orange Biscuits

5 1/2 c. sifted flour
1 heaping tsp. baking powder
1 tsp. salt
4 Tbs. sugar
3 Tbs. vegetable shortening
1 egg
1 c. milk
1 c. orange juice
2 dozen sugar cubes

Preheat oven to 375 degrees.
Mix together flour, baking powder, salt, sugar, and vegetable shortening and rub together like a pie crust. Mix egg and milk together. Add this to the flour and mix a little. Place mix on a flour-dusted board or table and roll dough out with a rolling pin 1/2-inch thick. Cut dough with a 2-inch cookie cutter and place biscuits close together on a greased cookie-sheet pan. Dip sugar cubes in the 1 cup of orange juice for a few seconds. Then place and press them somewhat in the center of the biscuits and bake them 14 to 20 minutes.
Yields 2 dozen biscuits

Party Date and Raisin Bread

1 lb. dates, (clean and cut up)
2 c. raisins (clean)
2 tsp. baking soda
2 c. hot water
2/3 c. margarine
2 c. sugar
1 tsp. vanilla
1 tsp. salt
2 eggs
6 level c. pastry flour
2 level tsp. baking powder
1 1/2 cup milk (or water)

Preheat oven to 350 degrees.
Put dates and raisins in a dish. Add baking soda and hot water. Let stand and cool. Mix margarine, sugar, vanilla, and salt well. Add eggs and beat for 3 minutes. Add dates, raisins, and their liquid. Mix a little. Add flour and baking powder, mix well at low speed. Add milk (or water). Put mix in well-greased round or bread pans and bake for about 45 to 50 minutes. Put a cookie-sheet pan over the mix for the first 15 minutes.
Yields 2 9- by 5-inch loaves.

Orange Date and Nut Bread

3/4 c. chopped dates
1 c. orange juice
1 c. sugar
1/4 c. butter
1 egg
1 tsp. salt
1 tsp. baking soda
3 c. all purpose flour
1 level tsp. baking powder
3/4 c. chopped pecans

Preheat oven to 350 degrees.
Soak chopped dates in the orange juice. Cream the sugar and butter. Add the egg, salt, baking soda, dates, and juice. Stir a little and then mix in the flour, baking powder, and pecans. Place mixture in a greased pan and bake for 25 to 30 minutes.
Yields 1 9- by 5-inch loaf

Whole Wheat Muffins

1 c. brown sugar
1/2 c. soybean or vegetable oil
1 tsp. salt
3 egg whites
1 c. milk
2 1/2 c. whole wheat flour
1 1/2 Tbs. baking powder
1 c. soft raisins

Preheat oven to 350 degrees.
Mix brown sugar, oil, and salt for 2 minutes. Add egg whites and milk and mix for 2 more minutes. Add whole wheat flour, baking powder, and raisins. Mix on low speed for 2 minutes. Spoon mixture into greased muffin tins, 2/3 full. Bake for 15 to 20 minutes. You can put paper liners into the muffin tins instead of greasing the muffin tins.
Yields 1 1/2 dozen muffins

Old-Fashioned Popovers

2 c. whole eggs
1 qt. whole milk
4 tsp. salt
4 1/2 c. bread flour

Preheat oven to 400 degrees.
Blend all together with a wire whip or mixer machine until nice and smooth. Fill mixture into well-greased muffin tins, 2/3 full. Give room to "pop-up." Bake until golden brown. Best when served hot and golden brown.
Yields about 4 dozen popovers

Fruit Party Bread or Muffins

1 c. sugar
1/3 c. butter
1 1/2 tsp. salt
1 tsp. baking soda
1 large egg
1 c. orange juice
1 c. chopped medium dates
    (or blueberries, or banana)
3 1/2 c. pastry flour

Preheat oven to 350 degrees.
Mix sugar, butter, salt, and baking soda at medium speed for 2 minutes. Add egg and mix for a minute. Then add the rest of the products, including the chopped dates (or blueberries, or sliced bananas) and mix a little. Place mix in a greased bread pan, 2/3 full. Bake fruit bread for 30 to 35 muffins for 15 to 20 minutes.
Yields one small loaf or 1 1/2 dozen muffins

Basic Mix for Cupcakes or Muffins

1 1/4 c. sugar
1/2 c. vegetable shortening
1 tsp. salt
1 tsp. nutmeg
1 tsp. lemon extract
3 whole eggs
1 c. milk
2 1/2 c. pastry flour
4 level tsp. baking powder

Preheat oven to 375 degrees.
Cream sugar, vegetable shortening, salt, nutmeg, and lemon extract for 3 minutes. Add eggs gradually and mix for 3 minutes, scraping the bowl often. Add milk and mix on low for 1 minute. Add flour and baking powder and mix for 2 minutes on low speed. Pour mixture into greased or paper-lined muffin tins, 2/3 full. Garnish with blueberries, chopped nuts, or streusel. Bake for about 12 minutes.
Yields 18 muffins or cupcakes

Holiday Fruit Bread

1 lb. raisins
2 1/2 c. chopped dates
2 1/2 c. hot water
2 c. sugar
1 c. vegetable shortening
3 eggs
16 maraschino cherries, chopped
1 (8 oz.) can pineapple tidbits
1 tsp. salt
4 level tsp. baking soda
1 tsp. vanilla
2 c. chopped pecans
5 1/2 c. pastry flour
1 tsp. baking powder

Preheat oven to 350 degrees.
Place raisins and chopped dates in hot water for 5 minutes. Mix sugar, vegetable shortening, and eggs for 2 minutes. Combine everything together, mixing the flour and baking powder last. Mix well for 2 minutes. Place mixture in 2 paper-lined, 9- by 5-inch bread pans and bake for 35 to 40 minutes.
Yields 2 loaves. Keeps well in the freezer.

Banana Nut Bread

1 3/4 c. sugar
2/3 c. vegetable shortening
4 beaten eggs
3 crushed bananas
3 Tbs. sour milk (or buttermilk)
1 Tbs. lemon juice
1 tsp. baking soda
3 c. flour
2 tsp. baking powder
1 Tbs. salt
1 1/2 c. chopped nuts

Preheat oven to 350 degrees.
Cream sugar and vegetable shortening, using a flat paddle at medium speed for 3 minutes. Add the beaten eggs and mix for 1 minute. Then add the crushed bananas and mix for 1 minute. Next add the sour milk and lemon juice. Add all the dry ingredients and nuts and mix for an additional 2 minutes. Place the batter in 2 greased 9- by 5-inch bread pans. Bake for 35 to 40 minutes. Keep cold for easier slicing.
Yields two loaves

Cinnamon Biscuits

Batter
4 1/2 c. all purpose flour
3 Tbs. baking powder
1/3 c. sugar
1 Tbs. salt
1/2 c. vegetable shortening
4 beaten eggs
1 1/4 c. milk

Filling
1 c. soft raisins
1 c. brown sugar
1 tsp. cinnamon
1/2 c. soft butter

Preheat oven to 400 degrees.
Mix flour, baking powder, sugar, and salt with vegetable shortening. Mix by hand as if making a pie crust. Combine beaten eggs with milk. Mix with dry ingredients by hand or mixer, slow speed, being careful not to overmix. Place dough on floured table and let rest for 10·minutes. While dough is resting, make the filling. Combine raisins, brown sugar, cinnamon, and soft butter. Blend all this together. Roll out the dough on a floured board— about 8 inches wide—and spread the filling over the dough and roll it up like a jelly roll. Cut the roll in 1/2-inch slices and place slices on a sheet pan. Bake 20 to 25 minutes.
Yields 2 dozen small biscuits

Coffee Cake

Cake Mix
1 c. sugar
2/3 c. vegetable shortening
1 tsp. salt
3 whole eggs
2 c. milk
4 1/2 c. flour
4 tsp. baking powder

Topping
1 c. granulated sugar
1/2 c. butter
3/4 c. flour
1 Tbs. cinnamon
1 tsp. salt

Preheat oven to 350 degrees.
Cream sugar, vegetable shortening, and salt for 3 minutes. Add eggs and mix for 3 minutes more. Add milk and mix on low for 1 minute. Add flour and baking powder and mix for 2 minutes on low speed. Pour mixture into a greased 9- by 14-inch cake pan. Blend topping ingredients together by hand until mix resembles coarse crumbs. Sprinkle over cake mixture. Bake for about 30 to 35 minutes.
Yields one 9- by 14-inch coffee cake

Blueberry Muffins

2 c. flour
1 Tbs. baking powder
3 Tbs. sugar
1 beaten egg
2 c. milk
1/4 c. melted butter
1 c. clean blueberries

Preheat oven to 375 degrees.
Combine flour, baking powder, and sugar in mixing bowl. Combine beaten egg, milk, and melted butter. Add milk mixture to flour mixture and mix a little. Gently mix in clean blueberries. Spoon batter into greased muffin tins, 2/3 full. Bake about 20 minutes until lightly brown.
Yields 12 to 15 muffins

Cake Type Biscuits

1/2 c. sugar
2/3 c. vegetable shortening
1 Tbs. salt
2 eggs
2 c. milk
6 c. flour
1 heaping Tbs. baking powder

Preheat oven to 375 degrees.
Mix sugar, vegetable shortening, and salt until creamy. Add the eggs and mix well. Add milk, mix a little, and add flour and baking powder and blend well. Do not overmix. Place on floured table and roll out 1/2-inch thick and cut out with a two-inch cutter. Place biscuits on a greased pan. Bake for 10 to 12 minutes, until golden brown.
Yields 4 dozen biscuits

Grandma's Corn Muffins

3 eggs
1/3 c. sugar
1 1/2 tsp. salt
1 c. milk
2 c. pastry flour
1 c. cornmeal
1 level Tbs. baking powder
1/4 c. soybean oil (or melted shortening)

Preheat oven to 375 degrees.
Beat eggs, sugar, and salt until light and foamy. Add milk and mix in all dry ingredients. Mix for 1 minute. Mix in soybean oil (or melted shortening). Spoon mixture into lightly greased muffin tins, filling 2/3 full. Bake for about 18 to 20 minutes.
Yields 2 dozen muffins

The Dearborn Inn was built in 1931 by Henry Ford I as a convenience to passengers and crews of planes arriving at Ford Flying Field, and also for visitors of Henry Ford Museum and Greenfield Village. Photograph courtesy of the Dearborn Inn

Hints on Cakemaking from Scratch

The ingredients must be pure and first class. Use powdered or fine sifted sugar. The flour should be pastry flour and sifted before using.

When a recipe calls for baking powder or cream of tartar, it should be sifted with the flour that is used. Baking soda should be dissolved in a little milk or water before using.

Eggs should be fresh and kept cool when separating the whites from the yolks. Care must be taken to have the former entirely free from the latter. As eggs differ in size, it is preferable to measure them first. Ten eggs are equal to one pint; eighteen egg whites are equal to one pint.

Fruits for cakes, such as raisins, currents, citrons, nuts, etc., must be clean and dusted with flour to prevent them from sinking to the bottom of the cake. Flavoring and spices should be of good quality and kept well corked or covered.

Note: *Unless otherwise stated, recipes call for 8-inch cake pans.*

To create a casual feeling, the Coffee Shop at the Dearborn Inn was paneled in knotty pine. Photograph courtesy of the Dearborn Inn

Butter Sponge Cake

8 whole eggs
1 1/3 c. sugar
1/2 level tsp. salt
1 tsp. lemon extract
2 c. sifted pastry flour
1/4 c. soybean (or bread) flour
1/4 c. melted butter

Preheat oven to 375 degrees.
Beat eggs and sugar over hot water bath until lukewarm. Remove from heat and continue beating until cool and very light. Add the flavoring. Incorporate the flours easily. Last of all, fold in the melted butter. Bake for about 20 minutes in 2 lightly greased and flour-dusted pans (or paper-lined pans).
Yields 2 8-inch layers

Devil's Food Cake
(Mrs. Ford's Favorite)

1 c. cocoa powder
1 c. sugar
1 c. hot milk
1 3/4 c. sugar
1 c. butter
5 eggs
1 level Tbs. baking soda
1/2 tsp. salt
1 tsp. vanilla
1 c. sour milk
4 c. pastry flour

Preheat oven to 350 degrees.
Combine the cocoa, 1 cup sugar, hot milk, and let cool for later use. Mix 1 3/4 cup sugar, butter, and eggs (2 at a time), slowly at second speed. Add baking soda, salt, and vanilla and mix for about 3 minutes. Add the sour milk and mix for another 30 seconds. Add the cooled mixture of cocoa, sugar, and milk. Last of all, mix in the flour. Bake in 2 8-inch layer pans for about 20 minutes. Cool the cake and frost with chocolate buttercream or chocolate icing.
Yields 2 8-inch layers

Coffee Cream Layer Cake

1 c. sugar
1/2 c. butter (or margarine)
1/2 tsp. salt
3 eggs
1/2 c. milk
2 tsp. vanilla
1 3/4 c. cake flour
1 tsp. baking powder

Preheat oven to 375 degrees.
Cream sugar, butter, (or margarine), and salt until fluffy. Scrape the bowl often. Add eggs (1 at a time) at medium speed. Scrape bowl. Add milk, vanilla, and dry ingredients. Mix until smooth. Pour mixture into 2 well-greased and floured 8-inch round cake tins. Bake for about 20 minutes. Fill with cream filling. Frost with frosting made with coffee instead of water.
Yields 2 8-inch layers

Silver White Cake

2 c. powdered sugar
1 c. vegetable shortening
1 tsp. salt
1/2 tsp. lemon extract
1 1/2 c. egg whites
2 c. flour
1 tsp. baking powder

Preheat oven to 350 degrees.
Cream together sugar, vegetable shortening, salt, and lemon extract for 3 minutes. Add egg whites (a little at a time), on second speed for about 5 minutes. Mix in flour and baking powder, (do not overmix). Place in greased 9- by 5-inch loaf or 2 8-inch round cake pans. Bake for 30 to 35 minutes.
Yields 1 loaf cake or 2 8-inch layers

Yellow Cake

2 c. pastry flour
1/2 c. cornstarch
2 level tsp. baking powder
1 1/2 c. sugar
2/3 c. butter (or margarine)
1/2 tsp. salt
4 eggs
1 tsp. vanilla extract
1/4 c. milk

Preheat oven to 350 degrees.
Blend together flour, cornstarch, and baking powder and set aside. Cream together the sugar, butter, and salt. Work the eggs in gradually. Add the vanilla, milk, and the flour mixture. Mix until smooth. Fill greased muffin tins half full or make a 2-layer cake from this mix. Bake for about 15 to 18 minutes.
Yields 2 8-inch layers or 18 cupcakes

Lady Werner's Cream Cheese Cake
(Boston Style)

1 c. soft cream cheese
1/3 c. sugar
1 tsp. lemon juice
2 c. whipped cream (or whipped topping)
9-inch graham cracker crust

Blend soft cream cheese, sugar, and lemon juice until creamy. Fold in two cups whipped cream (or whipped topping) by hand. Pour mixture into graham-cracker crust. Place in refrigerator to firm. Top with a cherry, strawberry, or pineapple filling.
Yields 1 9-inch cake

Grandma's Fruitcake

1 c. sugar
1 c. margarine
1/2 tsp. salt
6 whole eggs
1/3 c. milk
1 tsp. nutmeg
1 tsp. vanilla (or lemon) extract
1 c. chopped cherries
1 c. chopped pecans
1 c. chopped soft raisins
2 c. pastry flour
1 tsp. baking powder

Preheat oven to 350 degrees.
Place sugar, margarine, and salt together and mix until creamy. Add the eggs (two at a time). Mix until nice and creamy. Add the milk and flavoring and mix just a little. Add the chopped fruit and mix a little. Add the flour and baking powder and mix for 2 minutes. Place mix in a well-greased dusted or paper-lined 9- by 5-inch loaf pan and bake for about 35 to 40 minutes. Pierce the cake with a toothpick. The toothpick should come out clean when cake is done.
Yields one large fruitcake

Spicy Layer Cake or Cupcakes

1 1/3 c. brown sugar
1 c. margarine
1 Tbs. baking soda
1 level tsp. salt
3 large eggs
1 c. molasses
1 3/4 c. milk
4 1/2 c. pastry flour
1 tsp. cinnamon
1 tsp. allspice

Preheat oven to 375 degrees.
Mix at low speed the brown sugar, margarine, baking soda, and salt for 3 minutes. Mix in eggs (one at a time) for 3 minutes. Add molasses and mix a little. Scrape the bowl. Add the milk, flour, cinnamon, and allspice. Mix until smooth. Pour batter into 2 8-inch round greased cake tins. Bake for about 18 minutes until done. Another option is to pour mix into 24 greased muffin tins, 2/3 full, and bake the same way. When cool, decorate with chocolate icing or buttercream.
Yields 2 8-inch layers or 24 cupcakes

Holiday Fruitcake

2 1/2 c. sugar
2 c. butter
10 whole eggs
1 tsp. nutmeg
3 1/2 c. sifted cake flour
3 c. candied cherries, chopped in slices
1 1/2 c. candied citron thinly sliced

Preheat oven to 350 degrees.
Place sugar and butter in mixing bowl and beat until light and creamy. Add the eggs, a few at a time, and the nutmeg. Scrape the bowl. Add the sifted flour and mix lightly. Mix all the fruit and dust with a little flour to keep them from sinking to the bottom of the fruitcake. Mix thoroughly and pour into a paper-lined 9- by 5-inch loaf pan. Bake for 45 minutes. Pierce the cake with a toothpick. If the cake is baked, nothing will adhere to the toothpick.
Yields one large cake

Old-Fashioned Buttercream Frosting

3 c. powdered sugar
1/2 c. butter
1 tsp. vanilla extract
1/8 tsp. salt
1 egg white
1 Tbs. milk

Cream together sugar, butter, vanilla, salt, and egg white at medium speed until fluffy. Add milk and beat until nice and creamy. For decorating cupcakes, use a spatula.
Yields frosting for one large cake or 24 cupcakes

Plain Rich Piecrust

4 c. pastry flour
1 level tsp. baking powder
3 c. vegetable shortening
1 tsp. salt
5 tsp. sugar
3/4 c. cold water

Rub pastry flour, baking powder, vegetable shortening, salt, and sugar in a mixing bowl. Rub or mix by hand until coarse and crumbly. Then add water. Mix just a little. Do not overmix. It will make the piecrust tough. Place piecrust into a dish covered with a damp cloth. Place in refrigerator for later use. Yields 4 crusts for 2 double-crust pies

Regular Piecrust

11 c. pastry flour
1 tsp. baking powder
2 c. vegetable shortening
3 Tbs. salt
1/4 c. sugar
2 1/2 c. cold water

Place pastry flour, baking powder, vegetable shortening, salt, and sugar in a mixing bowl. Rub or mix by hand until coarse and crumbly. Then add water. Mix just a little. Do not overmix, it will make the piecrust tough. Place piecrust into a dish covered with a damp cloth. Place in refrigerator for later use. Yields 6 9-inch piecrusts for 3 double-crust pies.

Whole Wheat Piecrust

7 c. pastry flour
2 c. whole wheat flour
1 tsp. baking powder
3 c. vegetable shortening
2 Tbs. salt
2 1/2 c. cold water
4 Tbs. black molasses

Place pastry flour, whole wheat flour, baking powder, vegetable shortening, and salt in a mixing bowl. Mix or rub together well by hand until it feels and looks crumbly. Then add the water and molasses. Mix a little more, but not too much (it makes a crust tough). Place dough mix in a bowl and cover with a damp cloth. This dough keeps well in the refrigerator until needed.
Yields 5 9-inch piecrusts

Streusel Topping

Streusel is easy to make and nice to have on hand. It will keep well for weeks in the refrigerator. Streusel can be used for open-faced fruit pies, pandowdy topping, and bishop bread topping.

2 c. sugar
1 c. pastry flour
1 c. soft butter (or margarine)
1 tsp. cinnamon

Rub all ingredients together between your hands until it feels like coarse oatmeal. Use as needed. Keep some on hand in the refrigerator just in case you need a pandowdy in a hurry.

*Getting together for a family picture were, from right, Henry
Ford I, Clara (Bryant) Ford, and their son, Edsel Ford.
Photograph courtesy of the Henry Ford Museum Archives*

Fresh or Frozen Blueberry Pie

4 c. fresh or frozen blueberries
1 c. sugar
1/2 tsp. salt
1 Tbs. lemon juice
4 Tbs. minute tapioca

Preheat oven to 350 degrees.
Combine all ingredients. Let rest for about 15 minutes. Roll out pastry dough, fill with fruit filling, and cover with a top crust. Bake for about 30 to 35 minutes until nicely brown.

   To make blueberry pandowdy, put blueberry mixture in a small dish and top it with streusel. (See streusel topping recipe.) Bake for 25 minutes, cool, and top with whipped cream.
Yields 1 10-inch pie, or one pandowdy

Open-faced Fruit Pies

4 c. fresh fruit (apple, peach, rhubarb, blueberry, or cherry)
1 c. sugar
1/2 tsp. salt
1/2 tsp. cornstarch (optional)
1/2 tsp. nutmeg (or cinnamon)

Preheat oven to 350 degrees.
Mix fruit of your choice, sugar, salt, cornstarch, and nutmeg. If you use frozen fruit, let it come to room temperature, then add the sugar, salt, cornstarch, and nutmeg. Bake filling in a bottom-lined pastry shell, top it with streusel, and bake for 25 to 30 minutes until done. You may also bake without the streusel and top with whipped cream after the pie is baked.

Streusel Topping

1 c. soft brown sugar
3/4 c. pastry flour
1/2 c. butter (or margarine)
1/2 tsp. salt
1 tsp. cinnamon

Rub everything together between your hands, like crumb cake. Sprinkle on top of the fruit filling and bake 25 to 30 minutes, until a nice golden brown.
Yields enough for 1 10-inch pie

Double Crust Apple Pie

3 c. sliced fresh (or canned) apples
1 c. sugar
1/2 tsp. salt
1/2 tsp. nutmeg
2 Tbs. melted butter

Preheat oven to 400 degrees.
Mix everything together and place mix in bottom of prepared pie shell.
Wash edge of pie with brush and water. Roll top piecrust and put on filled
pie tin. Press edges a little and trim. Wash the top of the pie for a shiny glaze
with egg wash, or top with a little sugar for glaze. Bake for 25 to 30 minutes.
Yields 1 10-inch pie

Blueberry Pandowdy

4 c. fresh or frozen blueberries
1 1/2 c. sugar
1/2 tsp. nutmeg
1 Tbs. melted butter
1 1/2 c. fine bread (or cake) crumbs
1/2 c. water
1/2 tsp. grated lemon rind

Preheat oven to 325 degrees.
Mix all ingredients lightly. Put mixture in an 8- to 10-inch baking dish or pan
and cover with a good rich piecrust, or with a streusel mixture in place of the
piecrust. Bake for about 30 to 40 minutes.
Yields 1 10-inch pie

Pumpkin or Sweet Potato Pie

4 eggs
2 c. cooked mashed pumpkin (or mashed sweet potatoes)
3/4 c. sugar
1/2 tsp. salt
1/2 tsp. cinnamon (or nutmeg)
1/2 tsp. cloves (or ground ginger)
2 c. evaporated milk (or regular milk)

Preheat oven to 375 degrees.
Mix all ingredients and bake in an unbaked pie shell for 30 minutes, until set. (If you are not sure, take a toothpick and insert it in the center of the pie. If it comes out dry and clean the pie is done.)
Yields 1 9- or 10-inch pie

Fresh Rhubarb Pie
(Mrs. Ford's Favorite)

1 lb. rhubarb
12 oz. sugar
1 tsp. grated lemon rind
1 oz. cornstarch
pinch salt

Preheat oven to 375 degrees.
Young, tender rhubarb stalks usually require no peeling, but if necessary, peel off the outer layer of skin and cut into 1-inch pieces. Mix all ingredients well and fill a 10-inch pie shell. Wash the edge of the pie shell with a little water and cover with strips of pastry (or cover the entire pie). Bake for about 25 to 30 minutes.
Yields 1 10-inch pie

Banana or Coconut Cream Pie

3 whole eggs
3/4 c. sugar
1/4 tsp. salt
1 heaping tsp. cornstarch
1/4 tsp. nutmeg
1 tsp. vanilla extract
1/2 c. milk
2 c. milk
1 Tbs. butter
1 c. toasted coconut or 2 ripe sliced bananas
(dipped in a little lemon juice)

Mix well the eggs, sugar, salt, cornstarch, nutmeg, vanilla, and 1/2 cup of milk. Bring 2 cups of milk and butter to a boil. Add egg mixture to the boiling milk, stirring all the while until it is cooked. Stir in toasted coconut or sliced bananas. Place mixture in a 10-inch baked pie shell and top with whipped cream or meringue.
Yields 1 10-inch pie

Chocolate Cream Pie

3 whole eggs
1 c. sugar
1/2 tsp. salt
2 Tbs. cocoa powder
1/2 tsp. cinnamon
1 tsp. vanilla extract
1/2 c. lukewarm milk
2 c. milk
3 Tbs. butter (or margarine)

Mix eggs, sugar, salt, cocoa, cinnamon, vanilla, and 1/2 cup warm milk. Mix for a minute, until nice and smooth. Bring to a boil 2 cups of milk. Add butter (or margarine). Then add the egg mix slowly to the boiling milk, stirring while it is cooking for a minute until it is nice and smooth. Pour mixture into a 10-inch baked pie shell and top with whipped cream or meringue.
Yields 1 10-inch pie

Lemon Meringue Pie

Filling
2 Tbs. lemon rind
1 1/3 c. sugar
4 tsp. cornstarch
1/2 c. water
2 Tbs. lemon juice
2 egg yolks
1 1/2 c. water
2 Tbs. butter
1/8 tsp. salt

Meringue
2 egg whites
1/8 tsp. salt
1/4 c. sugar

Preheat oven to 375 degrees.
Filling
Grate the rind of the lemon into the sugar. Dissolve the cornstarch in the 1/2 cup of water, lemon juice, and egg yolks. Bring the 1 1/2 cups of water, sugar, lemon rind, butter, and salt to a boil. Add the dissolved cornstarch and egg yolks and cook until smooth and thick. Place mix in previously baked pie shell and top with meringue.

Meringue
Beat egg whites with salt until frothy. Add 1/4 cup of sugar and finish beating until stiff. Spread the meringue on the pie. Place the pie in oven for a few minutes until meringue browns some.
Yields 1 10-inch pie

Custard Pie or Cup Custard

6 eggs
3/4 c. sugar
1/8 tsp. salt
1/8 tsp. nutmeg
4 c. milk
1/8 tsp. vanilla extract

Preheat oven to 375 degrees.
Beat eggs, sugar, salt, and nutmeg for 2 minutes. Add the milk and vanilla. Mix again until smooth. Fill 9- or 10-inch unbaked pie shell and place pie in preheated oven. Bake pie until settled in center. Do not overbake custard. It will become watery or separated when overbaked.

Cup Custard
Fill cups with custard mix. Place cups in a dish or pan with 1/2 inch of water. Place this in the oven and bake until the custard is set in the center.
Yields one 9- or 10-inch pie or several cups

Boiled Pastry Cream

5 whole eggs
1/2 tsp. vanilla extract
1/2 tsp. cornstarch
1/4 tsp. salt
2/3 c. sugar
4 c. milk
1/2 c. butter

Mix the eggs, vanilla, cornstarch, salt, and the sugar. Beat for 2 minutes. Bring the milk and melted butter up to the boiling point. Add egg mix slowly to the milk and let cook for a minute. This mix can be used for cream puffs, eclairs, cream pies, coconut cream pies, and banana cream pies. Top pies with whipped cream.
Yields filling for 2 9-inch pies

Southern Pecan Pie

1/2 c. butter (or margarine)
1 c. granulated sugar
1/4 c. honey (or light corn syrup)
1/2 tsp. vanilla
1/2 tsp. salt
3 eggs slightly beaten
1 c. chopped pecans

Preheat oven to 350 degrees.
Cream butter and sugar. Add honey, vanilla, and salt. Blend well. Add slightly beaten eggs and blend. Pour mixture into unbaked pie shell. Last of all, add chopped pecans and bake for about 35 to 40 minutes.
Yields one 8-inch pie

Meringue for Pies and Tarts

6 whites of eggs
1 c. sugar
1/8 tsp. salt
1/8 tsp. cream of tartar
1/2 tsp. vanilla (or lemon extract)

Preheat oven to 375 degrees.
Place egg whites in clean bowl. Whip at high speed until foamy. Mix sugar, salt, and cream of tartar. Add this mix slowly to the foamy egg whites, continuing to whip at high speed until meringue stands up in dry peaks. Add a little vanilla or lemon extract. Spread on pie and bake for a few minutes until brown.
Yields topping for 2 pies

Sugar or Butter Cookies

2 c. granulated sugar
1 c. shortening (or butter)
2 tsp. salt
3 whole eggs
1/3 c. milk
1 tsp. lemon extract
3 c. pastry flour
4 tsp. baking powder

Preheat oven to 350 degrees.
Cream together sugar, shortening, and salt. Add eggs one at a time and cream well. Stir in the milk and lemon extract flavoring. Sift pastry flour and baking powder. Add this to the mixture until smooth. Roll out the dough 1/4-inch thick and sprinkle with coarse granulated sugar over the surface. Cut out with a cookie cutter and place on a cookie sheet. Bake for about 10 or 11 minutes.
Yields 3 to 4 dozen cookies (depending on size of cookie cutter).

Almond Butter Cookies
(Mr. Ford's Favorite)

1/2 c. almond paste
1 1/3 c. sugar
1 c. butter
3 whole eggs
1 tsp. salt
1 tsp. almond extract
1 Tbs. milk
2 2/3 c. pastry flour

Preheat oven to 350 degrees.
Mix together almond paste, sugar, and butter until smooth and light. Add the eggs one at a time. Add salt, almond, and milk. Then fold in the flour, but do not overmix. Roll dough on floured board 1/4-inch thick. Cut in various shapes and bake on lightly greased pans for 9 to 11 minutes, or until brown. Remove from pans while still warm.
Yields about 3 dozen cookies

Chinese Almond Cookies

2 c. sugar
1 c. margarine
4 whole eggs
1/8 tsp. almond extract
drops of yellow food coloring
3 c. pastry flour
1 tsp. baking soda
1 tsp. salt
1/2 c. sliced almonds
12 maraschino cherries

Preheat oven to 375 degrees.
Cream sugar and margarine until creamy. Add eggs and almond extract. Add a few drops of yellow food coloring. Beat until well mixed. Add all the dry ingredients and mix well. Place cookie mix in a pastry bag. Drop dough on lightly greased baking sheet. Decorate with sliced almonds and a piece of cherry. Bake for 9 to 12 minutes until golden brown. (Cookies look and taste something like macaroons.)
Yields 4 dozen cookies

Chocolate Chip Cookies
(Mr. Ford's Favorite)

1/2 c. white sugar
1 c. brown sugar
3/4 c. margarine or butter
1 tsp. baking soda
1/8 tsp. salt
1 tsp. vanilla
1 tsp. milk
2 whole eggs
2 1/2 c. pastry flour
3 c. chocolate chips

Preheat oven to 350 degrees.
Mix sugars, butter, baking soda, salt, and vanilla for 3 minutes. Add milk and eggs (one at a time) and mix for 1 minute until well blended. Blend in flour and chocolate chips. Drop mix by spoonfuls on greased and floured pans. Bake for about 10 minutes. Remove from pans while still warm.
Yields 4 1/2 dozen cookies

Grandma's Chocolate Chip Drop Cookies

1 1/2 c. brown sugar
1 c. margarine (or butter)
3/4 tsp. baking soda
1/8 tsp. salt
1 tsp. vanilla
3 whole eggs
3/4 c. milk
3 c. pastry flour
3 c. chocolate chips

Preheat oven to 350 degrees.
Mix sugar, butter, soda, salt, and vanilla for 3 minutes. Add eggs (one at a time) and mix at medium speed for 1 minute until well blended. Stir in milk, flour, and chocolate chips. Mix for 1 or 2 minutes. Use a pastry bag or drop cookie mix by spoonfuls on greased and floured baking pans. Bake for about 9 or 10 minutes.
Yields about 3 dozen cookies

Real Chocolate Party Cookies

1/2 c. white sugar
1 1/2 c. brown sugar
1 c. butter
1 tsp. baking soda
1 tsp. salt
1 tsp. vanilla extract
1 tsp. milk (or water)
2 eggs
2 1/2 c. flour
3 1/2 c. chopped chocolate or chips

Preheat oven to 350 degrees.
Mix sugars, butter, soda, salt, vanilla, and milk for 2 minutes. Add eggs (one at a time) and mix until well blended. Blend flour and chocolate chunks or chips. Use pastry bag or drop cookie mix by spoonfuls on a lightly greased pan and bake for about 10 minutes. Remove cookies while still warm for best results.
Yields 4 1/2 dozen cookies

Pecan Cookies

3/4 c. white sugar
3/4 c. brown sugar
1 1/2 c. shortening (or margarine)
1 tsp. cinnamon
1 tsp. baking soda
5 whole eggs
1/2 tsp. vanilla
1/2 c. milk
4 c. pastry flour
2 1/2 c. chopped pecans

Preheat oven to 375 degrees.
Cream sugars, shortening, and cinnamon for 1 minute. Add baking soda and mix until light and creamy. Add the eggs, vanilla, and milk. Mix a little. Then add the flour and chopped pecans. Form dough into rolls about 2 inches thick and wrap in waxed paper to chill overnight. Slice dough 1/4-inch thick. Place cookies on a lightly greased (or paper-lined) pan. Bake about 10 minutes.
Yields about 4 dozen cookies

Fudge Brownies
(Mrs. Ford's Favorite)

2/3 c. bittersweet (or sweet) chocolate chips
3/4 c. butter
5 whole eggs
2 c. sugar
1 tsp. vanilla
1/8 tsp. salt
1/4 c. milk
2 3/4 c. pastry flour
1/2 tsp. baking powder
1 1/2 c. chopped pecans
1/4 c. milk

Preheat oven to 350 degrees.
Melt chocolate and butter in a double boiler and set aside to cool. Place eggs, sugar, vanilla, salt, and 1/4 cup milk in a mixing machine with a wire whip. Mix for 5 minutes at high speed. Blend in the melted chocolate mixture. Mix and blend in the pastry flour, baking powder, and chopped pecans. Add 1/4 cup milk. Pour mixture in a greased and floured 10-inch square pan. Bake for about 20 minutes.
Yields about 20, depending on size

Ladyfingers

4 clean egg whites
1/2 c. granulated sugar
1/8 tsp. salt
4 egg yolks
1/2 tsp. vanilla extract
1 level c. flour

Preheat oven to 400 degrees.
Beat egg whites until foamy. Slowly add sugar and salt. Beat to a stiff peak. Beat egg yolks in a separate bowl and fold into mixture. Add vanilla extract. Sift flour and fold carefully into mixture. Place mixture into pastry bag with plain tube. Press into finger shapes on paper-lined sheet pans. Dust with confectioners' sugar and bake immediately for 7 to 10 minutes.
Yields 3 dozen ladyfingers

Honey Wafer Roll-Ups
One of Mrs. Ford's Party Cookies

1 c. sugar
8 oz. butter
1 tsp. lemon extract
2 c. honey
1/2 tsp. salt
4 eggs
8 c. pastry flour

Preheat oven to 350 degrees.
Mix sugar, butter, lemon extract, honey, and salt for 2 minutes. Then add eggs, 2 at a time. Mix 1 minute after each addition. Add the flour gradually. Drop the mixture with a tablespoon on a well-greased pan (far apart). Bake in a medium oven 7 to 8 minutes. When done, roll while still warm on a pencil or round stick to cool. Brandy wafers can be made by adding brandy in place of lemon extract.
Yields 8 dozen cookies

Speculaas (St. Nicholas) Cookies

3 c. brown sugar
1 c. butter
2 whole eggs
1/2 c. sour milk
3 1/2 c. all purpose flour
1 Tbs. ground cinnamon
1 tsp. nutmeg
1 tsp. baking soda
1 tsp. salt
1/2 tsp. ground cloves
2 1/2 c. sliced almonds (or chopped pecans)

Cream sugar and butter for 3 minutes. Add eggs and mix. Scrape bowl and add sour milk. Mix a little, then add the flour, spices, and nuts. Mix thoroughly. Place mix on floured table. Divide into rolls, each 8 inches long by 1 inch thick. Wrap in waxed paper and refrigerate overnight, or longer. When needed, slice into 1/4-inch thick slices and bake at 350 degees for 8 to 10 minutes. The cookies will spread some.
Yields about 4 to 5 dozen cookies

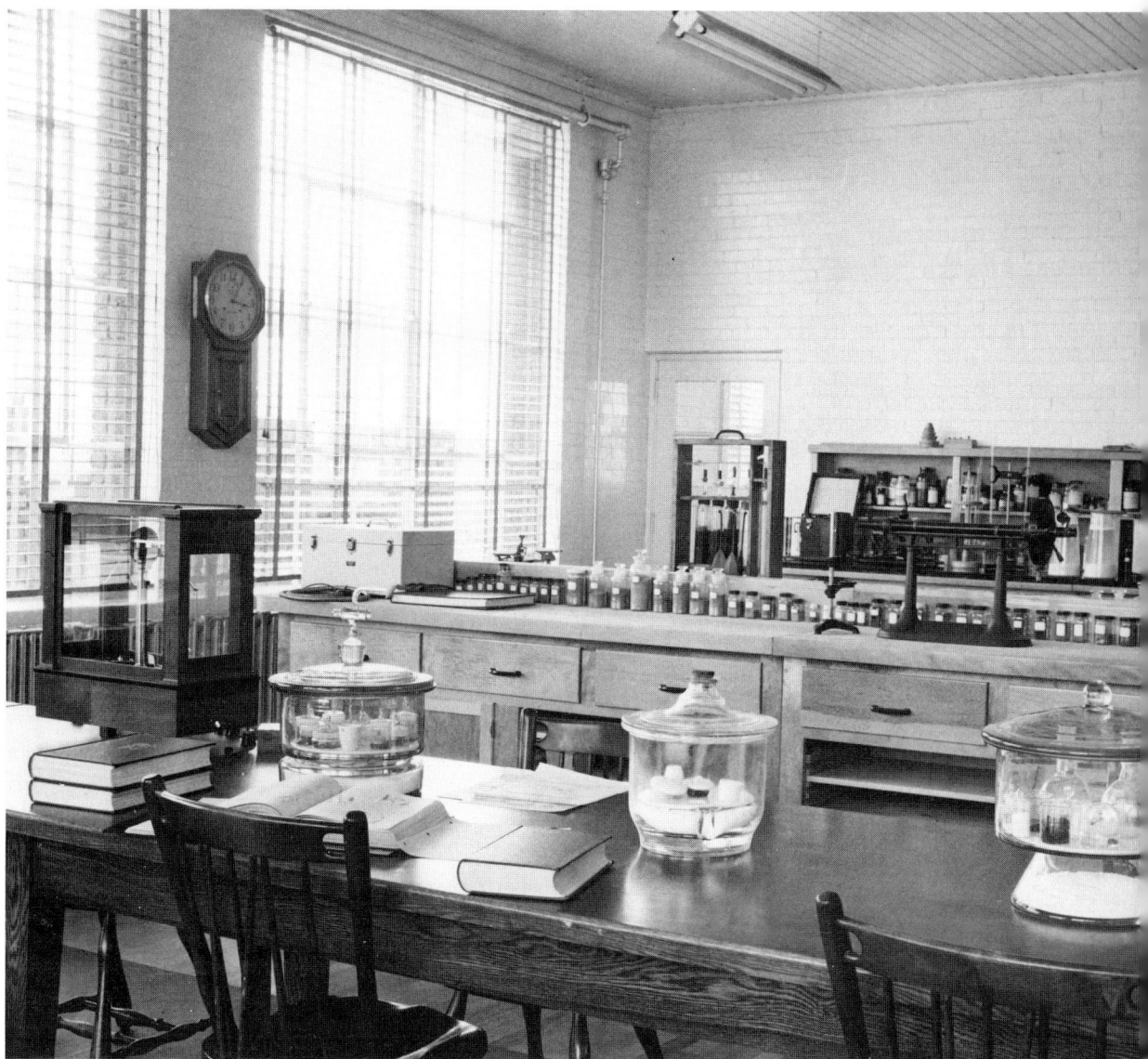

Pictured is the interior of the Carver Laboratory
when it was used for soybean research. Photograph
courtesy of the Henry Ford Museum Archives

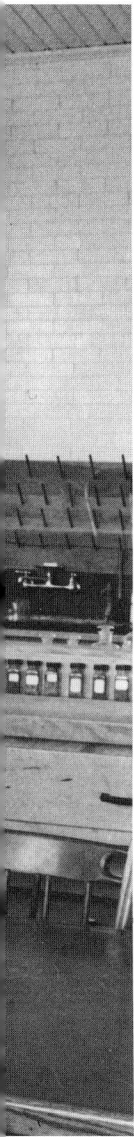

P A R T I I
Mr. Ford Introduces Me to the Soybean

In 1934, at Mr. Ford's request, I started experimenting with soybeans. Dr. Ruddiman had the miller send me samples of soybean flour. I started by making soft rolls, and then began trying many different things.

Always what I made had to be approved by Dr. Ruddiman before I could send it to the Ford family. However, it could be served at the Dearborn Inn without his approval. I made many recipes in five or six months, and as far as I know, no other soy recipes were around.

Mr. Ford saw the possibility for the use of soybeans in food, milk and ice cream, paint, plastics, and many other things before 1930. In his fast-growing automobile industry, and since, the soybean has played a big part in the manufacturing of commercial products.

While I researched food recipes with soybeans, Dr. Ruddiman and chemist Bob Smith experimented with making a substitute for milk and ice cream from the beans. The first products were served at the Dearborn Inn, but weren't well liked. However, a Del Soy (*Del*icious *Soy*bean) topping was very tasty and is still in use.

Robert Boyer, another chemist, created the first car body part of plastic made from the soybean. Several other soybean researchers I remember were R. H. McCarroll and Harold Joyce.

Mr. Ford was a friend of George Washington Carver, the black botanical chemist who was director of research in 1936 at Tuskegee Institute in Alabama. Dr. Carver had researched the peanut and found three hundred commercial uses for it. He and his assistant, Austin Curtis, were also trying to make a rubber substitute, but weren't successful at that.

Mr. Curtis spent the summer of 1940 in Dearborn working with Robert Boyer in the soybean laboratory. Dr. Carver planned to visit for several weeks in 1942. Mr. Ford was so pleased about that he had the old Dearborn Waterworks made over into a laboratory for Dr. Carver's use. After Dr. Carver's death several years later, Mr. Ford named the building the Carver Laboratory.

I had worked as pastry chef at the Dearborn Inn until 1932. Then I went into Dr. Ruddiman's laboratory in Greenfield Village. This soybean experimenting was a sideline, you might say. It started small but grew to be very important to Mr. Ford. He wanted more and more food made with the soybean.

Clara Ford was not as interested in the soybean as her husband, but she especially liked some soybean food such as cookies made with white chocolate chips, and soy bread. She wanted the bread sent to the mansion every day.

A favorite of Mr. Ford's was a soybean cracker that he named the Model T. He gave it that name because I cut the crackers out of the dough with a Model T hubcap. You see, there were no cookie cutters to suit the purpose, so I cleaned up a hubcap and used it. It worked just fine. I still have the original hubcap that Mr. Ford gave me.

About Soybeans

Soybeans are rich in protein and oil. They contain an average of thirty-five percent protein, eighteen to twenty percent oil, one to three percent lecithin, no starch (but a little sugar), a fair supply of vitamins and a fair amount of mineral salts. They are an especially good source of vitamins A and B. The soybean is a nearly complete food supplement and could sustain life for a long time.

Soy flour (ground defatted soybeans) is about ten times as rich in minerals as wheat flour, fifteen times as rich in lime, eight times as rich in phosphorous and ten times as rich in oil.

Soybean flour is creamy in color, fluffy and fascinating to work with. It is not really a flour as are grain flour and potato flour. It is more on the order of powdered milk and powdered eggs in use and in concentration of food value, and it is an economical way of stepping up the protein content of any baked product. Soybean-flour baked products stay fresh longer, toast better, and have a delicious nutlike flavor.

Soybean flour is commonly used to boost the nutritional value of ice cream, cakes, cookies, waffles, pancakes, rolls, bread, and other foods that will be thoroughly baked or cooked. Soybean powder (heat treated) is useful as a protein boost in foods that will be minimally cooked.

Soybean milk, a drink made from cooked soybeans, is especially useful for children with allergies. Soy nuts (deep fried in soybean oil) or roasted soybeans can be eaten as snacks and contain even more protein than peanuts.

The whole soybean is but one way to consume soy protein and probably not the most popular way at that. There are soybean grits that can be cooked as cereal or eaten as a side dish or used for stuffing, and soybean flakes (dry roasted soybeans) that have been flattened and cut and can be cooked as a cereal.

About eighty percent of commercial salad dressings, margarine, and mayonnaise are made from soybean oil extracted from the bean with the protein-rich residue. Many cooking and salad oils are all or part soybean oil as well.

When you buy soybean margarine or other vegetable shortenings made from soybean oil choose the one that lists soybean oil as the first ingredient. It will be the least saturated.

Note: *Supermarkets and some grocery stores carry some soybean products, but if you can't find what you need, try a health food store.*

The Carver Laboratory was used for soybean research when this picture was taken in 1942. Formerly, the building had been the water-works for the Village of Dearborn. At present it houses a restaurant. Photograph courtesy of the Henry Ford Museum Archives

S O Y B E A N R E C I P E S

A Model T hubcap is included in this picture of Model T soybean crackers. Photograph by Eleanor Eaton

Model T. Crackers
(Mr. Ford's Favorite)

1 c. pastry flour
1 c. soybean flour
1 c. whole wheat flour
2 Tbs. baking powder
1 Tbs. salt
2 c. sugar
1 c. soft soybean margarine
1 c. soybean milk
   (or regular milk)
1 Tbs. wheat germ

Preheat oven to 350 degrees.

Mix all flours, baking powder, salt, sugar, and margarine together, rubbing it between your hands as you would for piecrust. Add all the milk, and mix a little. Place dough on worktable, roll it out 1/8-inch thick. Sprinkle with some wheat germ. Cut with clean Model T hubcap (or 2- or 3-inch cookie cutter). Place on baking sheet, prick with fork 3 or 4 times. Bake for about 10 to 12 minutes. Serve with soup, salad, or cheese.

Yields about 4 dozen crackers

The design of the hubcap is shown actual size. I used the hubcap to cut out the crackers—thus their name. Drawing by Virginia Eaton

Soy Bread Homemade Style

1/3 c. soy margarine
2 tsp. salt
1/4 c. sugar (or honey)
1 oz. yeast cake
2 cups warm milk
3 1/2 c. bread flour
1 c. soy flour

Preheat oven to 350 degrees. Mix soy margarine, salt, and sugar (or honey). Add dissolved yeast and milk. Then add flours. Knead well to make a fairly stiff dough. Cover and let rise to double in size. Knead again and shape into one large or two small loaves. When double in volume, bake in a moderate oven. Be careful, this bread browns very quickly.
Yields one large or two small loaves

Soy Whole Wheat Bread

1 c. brown sugar
1/4 c. soy margarine
1 1/2 tsp. salt
3 eggs
2 c. sour milk
1 Tbs. baking soda
1/2 c. molasses
2 1/2 c. whole wheat flour
1 c. soybean flour

A soybean bouquet

Preheat oven to 350 degrees.
Mix sugar, soy margarine, and salt using a mixer with a flat paddle for 2 minutes. Add eggs and mix for 2 more minutes. Mix in sour milk, soda, and molasses and mix for 1 minute. Add whole wheat flour and soybean flour and mix at low speed for 2 minutes. Place batter in 2 greased 9- by 5-inch loaf pans. Bake for 35 to 40 minutes.
Yields two 9- by 5-inch loaves

Basic Soy Muffin Mix

5 c. sugar
1/2 lb. soy margarine
5 eggs
2 c. soy milk (or regular)
1 Tbs. salt
1 tsp. nutmeg
1 tsp. lemon extract
4 c. pastry flour
2/3 c. soybean flour
4 Tbs. baking powder
1 c. blueberries, (or other fruit)

Preheat oven to 375 degrees.
Cream sugar and margarine for 4 minutes, then add the eggs gradually, scraping the bowl. Add the milk, flavorings, and spice and mix a little. Add the pastry flour, soy flour, and baking powder. Blend well. Mix in blueberries (or any fruit), and fill muffin tins 2/3 full and garnish top with blueberries (or any fruit), and bake for 15 minutes, or until golden brown and done.
Yields 4 dozen cupcakes or muffins

Soybean Yellow Cake

1 c. sugar
1 c. soy margarine
1 tsp. salt
1 tsp. lemon extract
1/2 tsp. nutmeg
4 eggs
1/2 c. soy milk (or regular)
1 c. pastry flour
1/2 c. soybean flour
1 Tbs. baking powder

Preheat oven to 350 degrees.
Mix sugar, soy margarine, salt, lemon extract, and nutmeg for 3 minutes. Add the eggs (two at a time) and mix for 3 minutes. Scrape the bowl. Add the milk and mix a little. Add the flours, and baking powder. Mix well. Place mixture in paper-lined cake pans or in greased muffin tins. Bake for about 20 to 25 minutes.
Yields 2 8-inch layers or 18 cupcakes

Soybean Sponge Cake

8 c. whole eggs
1 1/8 c. sugar
1/2 tsp. salt
1/3 tsp. lemon extract
1/2 c. soybean flour
1 1/2 c. bread flour
1 tsp. baking soda
2 oz. melted soybean margarine (or butter)

Preheat oven to 350 degrees.
Beat eggs, sugar, and salt at high speed until very light (approximately 10 minutes). Add lemon extract. Fold in flours and baking soda by hand (do not overmix). Last of all fold in the melted soybean margarine (or butter). Bake for 20 minutes in a lightly greased and flour-dusted angel food cake pan.
Yields 1 9- by 5-inch cake

Soybean Oatmeal Pancakes or Waffles

3 egg whites
1 tsp. salt
1/3 c. honey (or sugar)
1 3/4 c. milk
1/2 c. soybean oil (or melted soy margarine)
3/4 c. soybean flour
1 c. whole wheat flour
3/4 c. instant rolled oats
1 Tbs. baking soda

Beat the egg whites, salt, and honey (or sugar) until foamy. Add the milk and oil and stir a little. Then fold in the flours, rolled oats, and baking soda. Heat a greased skillet to about 350 degrees. Pour 2-ounce pancakes, cook until they bubble, turn and brown the other side. Serve with honey or syrup.
Yields 3 1/2 dozen 2-ounce pancakes

Soybean Flour Pie Dough

10 oz. soy margarine
4 c. pastry flour
3/4 c. soybean flour
2 tsp. salt
2 Tbs. sugar
1 tsp. baking soda
1 1/8 c. cold water

Rub or fold margarine into flours. Add salt, sugar, and baking soda and mix a little more. Add cold water, mix a very little more (do not overmix). Place mixed piecrust into a pan and cover with a damp cloth. Place in refrigerator for later use. This pie dough will keep in the refrigerator for a couple of weeks. It is nice to have on hand when needed.
Yields 4 single 9-inch shells

Rich Soy Piecrust

2 c. pastry flour
1 c. soybean flour
1 tsp. baking soda
2/3 c. sugar
1/3 tsp. salt
1 c. soy margarine
1/3 c. soy milk (or water)

Rub together by hand or machine the flours, baking soda, sugar, salt, and margarine until crumbly. Add soy milk (or water). Mix just a little. Makes a very good piecrust.
Yields 4 single 9-inch piecrusts

Graham Cracker Crust

1 c. graham cracker crumbs
1/3 c. brown sugar
pinch salt
1/2 c. soybean oil
1 tsp. vanilla

Preheat oven to 350 degrees.
Combine graham cracker crumbs, sugar, salt, soybean oil, and vanilla. Rub mixture together and spread on bottom of two 9-inch pie tins (or one 14-inch cake pan. Bake for 8 minutes and you have a shell or bottom for a favorite pie or cake.
Yields two 9-inch piecrusts or one 14-inch cake bottom

Soybean Whole Wheat Piecrust

4 c. whole wheat flour
2 c. soybean flour
3 tsp. salt
1 1/2 lb. soybean margarine
2 1/4 c. cold water
1/2 tsp. baking soda
3 Tbs. molasses

Rub or fold flours, salt, and soy margarine until mixture looks crumbly, like coarse oatmeal. Add the water, baking soda, and molasses. Mix just a little, (don't overmix). Place dough in the refrigerator, covered with a damp cloth, until needed.
Yields 6 9-inch single piecrusts

Soy Bread Pudding with Prunes and Raisins

4 eggs
1/2 c. sugar
1 tsp. cinnamon
2 tsp. salt
2 c. soy milk (or regular milk)
2 c. prune juice
2 cups diced, toasted soy bread
2 c. cooked (or canned) prunes
2 c. cleaned raisins

Preheat oven to 350 degrees.
Beat eggs, sugar, cinnamon, salt, and a little of the juice and milk. Add remainder of juice and milk and mix well. Place the toasted bread cubes, prunes, and raisins in a buttered dish and pour mixture over the cubes. Bake for about 30 to 35 minutes. Serve with sauce or whipped cream.
Yields one 10- by 12-inch dish

Soy Milk Custard Pie

6 eggs
1/3 c. sugar
1/2 tsp. salt
1 tsp. vanilla
1 Tbs. cornstarch
1 tsp. nutmeg
1 qt. soybean milk (or regular milk)

Preheat oven to 375 degrees.
Beat eggs, sugar, salt, and vanilla together very well. Add the cornstarch, nutmeg, and soy milk and mix well until smooth. If lumpy, strain through a fine sieve. Pour mixture into an unbaked pie shell or 8 cups for cup custard. Bake (placing cups in a pan with some water) until set in the center, approximately 35 minutes.
Yields 1 9-inch pie or 8 cup custards

White Chocolate Soybean Cookies
(One of Mrs. Ford's Favorites)

1 3/4 c. brown sugar
1 c. soy margarine
1 tsp. salt
1 tsp. baking soda
1 tsp. vanilla extract
2 eggs
1 Tbs. soy milk (or water)
1 c. pastry flour
3/4 soybean flour
2 1/2 c. white chocolate chips
2/3 c. crushed roasted soybeans

Preheat oven to 375 degrees.
Mix sugar, soy margarine, salt, baking soda, and vanilla for 1 minute. Add eggs and soy milk. Mix a little. Add flours, white chocolate chips, and crushed soybeans. Mix a little. Drop 2 inches apart from pastry bag or teaspoon on a well-greased baking pan. Bake for about 8 to 10 minutes until golden brown. Remove from baking pan while still warm.
Yields 5 dozen cookies

Coconut Soy Cookies

2 1/4 c. sugar
1/2 lb. soybean margarine
4 eggs
1/3 c. soy milk
2 c. pastry flour
1/4 c. soy flour (or whole wheat flour)
1 grated lemon rind and juice
1 tsp. salt
1 tsp. baking soda
2 c. lightly toasted coconut

Preheat oven to 325 degrees.
Cream sugar and margarine until light. Add the eggs (one at a time) and mix well. Add milk and mix a little. Add flours, lemon rind and juice, salt, and baking soda. Mix a little. Put mix in a pastry bag. Make round cookies or ladyfingers. Sprinkle coconut on top before baking and bake for about 8 to 10 minutes.
Yields 3 dozen cookies

Soybean Macaroons

8 oz. fine granulated sugar
1/4 c. soybean flour
1 tsp. salt
4 egg whites
8 oz. almond paste
1/2 tsp. lemon (or almond) extract
1 c. roasted soybeans

Preheat oven to 350 degrees.
Combine dry ingredients. Add egg whites two at a time. Add almond paste. Mix for three or four minutes. Add the almond (or lemon) extract and mix until you have a nice smooth dough. Place dough in a pastry bag with plain or a star tube. Press the dough from the bag on a lightly greased sheet pan and decorate with roasted soybeans. Bake cookies for 10 to 13 minutes until golden brown.
Yields 18 to 24 cookies

Chinese Almond Soybean Cookies

2 c. sugar
1 c. soy margarine
4 eggs
1/8 tsp. almond extract (or lemon extract)
drops of yellow food coloring
3 c. pastry flour
1 tsp. baking powder
1 tsp. salt
1/2 c. sliced almonds
12 maraschino cherries

Preheat oven to 375 degrees.
Cream sugar and margarine until creamy. Add eggs (two at a time), almond extract, and a few drops of food coloring. Beat until well mixed. Add flour, baking powder, and salt and mix well. Place cookie mix in a pastry bag. Drop dough on lightly greased baking sheet. Decorate with sliced almonds and a piece of cherry. Bake for 9 to 12 minutes until golden brown. (Cookies look and taste something like macaroons.)
Yields 3 dozen cookies

Sugar Soybean Cookies

1 1/4 c. granulated sugar
2/3 c. soybean margarine
1 tsp. salt
1/2 tsp. baking soda
2 eggs
2 Tbs. soybean milk (or water)
1 tsp. vanilla
1 3/4 c. pastry flour
1/4 c. soybean flour (or wheat germ)
maraschino cherries
unsalted, roasted soybeans or sliced almonds

Preheat oven to 350 degrees.
Cream sugar, margarine, salt, and baking soda until fluffy. Beat in the eggs at medium speed for 2 minutes. Add milk, vanilla, and the flours. Mix for 1 minute. Place mixture in a pastry bag with a plain (or star-shaped) tube. Press the dough from the bag onto a paper-lined sheet or greased, floured cookie pans and decorate with a piece of cherry and some sliced almonds or unsalted soy beans. Bake the cookies for 10 to 13 minutes.
Yields about 2 dozen cookies

Soybean Cookies

1 c. brown sugar
3/4 c. margarine
3 eggs
1 tsp. salt
1/2 tsp. nutmeg
1 tsp. lemon rind and juice
1/3 c. soy milk (or regular milk)
1 3/4 c. pastry flour
1/3 c. soy flour (or whole wheat flour)
1/2 tsp. baking soda

Preheat oven to 350 degrees.
Cream sugar and margarine well. Add eggs (one at a time). Mix well. Add salt, nutmeg, grated lemon peel and juice, and soy milk and mix a little. Add flours. Mix a little. Use pastry bag or spoon mixture onto lightly greased pans. Bake for about 10 minutes.
Yields about 3 dozen cookies

Soy Butter Cookies

1 1/2 c. soy margarine
1 1/3 c. brown sugar
3 eggs
1/4 c. milk
2 tsp. lemon juice
1 tsp. lemon rind
1 tsp. nutmeg (or mace)
1 tsp. salt
1 tsp. baking soda
1 1/2 c. pastry flour
1/4 c. soy flour (or whole wheat flour)

Preheat oven to 350 degrees.
Mix margarine and brown sugar for 2 minutes. Add the eggs and mix for 2 more minutes. Scrape bowl and add the milk, lemon juice and lemon rind and mix for 1 minute. Mix nutmeg, salt, baking soda, and flours, and mix for 2 minutes. Drop cookie dough by spoonfuls onto a greased cookie sheet and bake for about 10 minutes. Or roll the cookie dough in waxed paper in 1/2-inch-thick rolls and place in the refrigerator overnight. Unwrap and slice into thin slices and bake. The mix can also be spread out on a sheet-cake pan and baked for about 10 minutes and cut into bars after they are cooled.
Yields 2 1/2 dozen cookies

Chocolate Chip Soybean Cookies
(Made Especially for Mr. Ford)

3 c. soft brown sugar
2 c. soy margarine
4 eggs
1 tsp. salt
1 tsp. vanilla extract
2 tsp. baking soda
2 Tbs. milk
3 c. pastry flour
1 c. soybean flour (or bread flour)
2 c. crushed roasted soybean nuts (unsalted)
4 c. chocolate chips

Preheat oven to 350 degrees.
Mix soft brown sugar and margarine. Mix for 2 minutes. Add eggs, two at a time, mix for about 3 or 4 minutes. Add salt, vanilla, baking soda, milk, and flours. Mix a little—5 or 6 turns. Mix in roasted soybeans and chocolate chips. Mix a little. Put some mix in a pastry bag and squeeze mix onto greased pans. This should be about the size of a half-dollar. Flatten the top and brush with an egg wash. Bake for about 8 to 10 minutes.
Yields 10 dozen cookies

Soybean Apple Salad

1 c. well-cooked soybeans (or roasted soybeans)
1 c. diced chopped apples
1 c. clean washed raisins
1 c. finely chopped celery
1 c. clean grated carrots
1 c. soybean salad dressing
salt to taste
French dressing (or your favorite dressing)

Toss all ingredients together including Soybean Salad dressing and chill in the refrigerator. Serve on leaf lettuce. Top with thin green pepper ring and French dressing (or your favorite dressing).
Yields 8 generous servings

Soybean Sprout Salad

1 c. shredded lettuce
1 c. grated carrots
1 c. fine chopped celery
1 c. soybean sprouts
1 ripe tomato (sliced or cubed)
French dressing (or soybean oil)
salt
chopped parsley

Toss first 5 ingredients together. Moisten with some French dressing (or some pure soybean oil). Add salt to taste. Top with chopped parsley.
Yields 4 or 5 servings.

Green Goddess Soybean Dressing

1/2 c. chopped parsley
1/2 c. chopped watercress
4 Tbs. tarragon vinegar
2 Tbs. anchovy paste
2 Tbs. chopped chives
2 Tbs. soybean oil

Combine parsley, watercress, vinegar, anchovy paste, chives, and soybean oil. Place in blender at high speed for 1 minute until smooth. Keeps well in the refrigerator.
Yields 1 1/2 cups dressing

Basic Soy Oil Dressing

1/3 c. vinegar
1 tsp. salt
1/2 tsp. pepper
1 Tbs. sugar
1 Tbs. dry mustard
1 c. soybean oil

Combine first five ingredients in a mixing bowl using wire whip. Turn on mixer to low speed and add oil in a thin stream for 2 minutes. Mix again before serving, or use as a base for additional recipes.
Yields 1 1/2 cups dressing

Honey Soy Oil Dressing

1/2 c. lemon juice
1/2 c. soy oil
3 Tbs. honey
pinch salt

Mix thoroughly and serve on green salads. Will refrigerate very well.
Yields 1 1/2 cups dressing

Soy Oil Dressing

1/2 c. wine vinegar
1 tsp. dry mustard
1 c. soybean oil
salt
pepper
garlic

Mix vinegar and mustard. Add soybean oil, salt, pepper, and garlic to taste. Mix thoroughly and serve over fresh crisp salad greens.
Yields 1 1/2 cups dressing

Vegetable Soybean Soup

1 c. diced green pepper
1 c. diced onions
1 c. diced celery
1/2 c. soy oil
2 c. cooked soft soybeans (or 2 c. canned soy beans)
3 c. water
1 tsp. salt
1/2 tsp. curry powder
2 1/2 c. diced tomatoes

Sauté green peppers, diced onions, and diced celery in soybean oil. When tender, combine with remaining ingredients and simmer for 20 minutes. Serve with soybean bread toast or soybean croutons.
Yields 8 or 9 servings

Soybean Carrot Soup

1 c. diced carrots
1 stalk diced celery
1 small diced onion
1 tsp. salt
1/3 tsp. pepper
4 c. water
1/2 c. mashed cooked soybeans (or canned soybeans)
2 Tbs. chopped parsley

Cook carrots, celery, onion, salt, and pepper in water until tender. Add mashed soybeans. Serve hot, topped with chopped parsley.
Yields 5 or 6 servings

Henry Ford is shown with George Washington Carver, botanical chemist of renown, who did some soybean research for Mr. Ford. Photograph courtesy of Jan Willemse

MENU
of
Dinner Served at Ford Exhibit
Century of Progress

August 17, 1934

∽

TOMATO JUICE SEASONED WITH SOY BEAN SAUCE

SALTED SOY BEANS

CELERY STUFFED WITH SOY BEAN CHEESE

PUREE OF SOY BEAN

SOY BEAN CRACKER

SOY BEAN CROQUETTES WITH TOMATO SAUCE

BUTTERED GREEN SOY BEANS

PINEAPPLE RING WITH SOY BEAN CHEESE
AND
SOY BEAN DRESSING

SOY BEAN BREAD WITH SOY BEAN RELISH

SOY BEAN MACAROONS

APPLE PIE (SOY BEAN CRUST)

COCOA WITH SOY BEAN MILK

SOY BEAN COFFEE

ASSORTED SOY BEAN COOKIES

SOY BEAN CAKES

ASSORTED SOY BEAN CANDY

Baked Soybeans

2 c. soybeans
2 Tbs. cornstarch
1/2 tsp. celery seed
1 1/2 tsp. salt
pinch paprika
1 tsp. onion juice
1 c. strained tomato pulp

Preheat oven to 350 degrees.
Boil soybeans, covered with water (at least an hour), until soft. Set aside.
Make a tomato sauce by mixing the cornstarch, celery seed, salt, paprika,
and onion juice with cold tomato pulp and cook until thickened. Pour over
the soft-cooked beans and bake in moderate oven until brown.
Yields 3 to 4 servings

Baked Soybeans Boston Style

1 lb. soybeans (cooked soft)
1 tsp. baking soda
1 Tbs. brown sugar
1 Tbs. molasses
2 tsp. salt
1 tsp. dry mustard
1/4 lb. diced salt pork

Soak the soybeans overnight in enough cold water to cover. Pour off the
water, add the soda, and cook gently until the beans are slightly softened.
Drain and reserve water. Mix the brown sugar, molasses, salt, and mustard
with a pint of the reserved cooking water and pour over the beans, adding
more water if the beans are not covered. Place the pork on the beans, cover,
and bring to a boil. Bake 2 hours at 300 degrees or until done. Slow baking
gives the beans a fine flavor.
Yields about 4 servings

(Opposite page) I planned this menu of all
soybean food that was served at a dinner at
the Ford Exhibit, Century of Progress in
Chicago, Illinois, August 17, 1934.
Photograph courtesy of Jan Willemse

Baked Soybeans Texas Style

8 c. cooked soybeans (or canned)
1/2 lb. diced salt pork (or diced bacon)
1 tsp. baking soda
1 Tbs. prepared mustard
4 Tbs. molasses

Preheat oven to 325 degrees.
Put the cooked soybeans, diced pork (or bacon), baking soda, mustard, and molasses in a bean pot with enough water to cover and bake in slow oven for 1 hour or until done. Cover bean pot and add additional water if needed. Don't let soybeans get dry.
Yields 6 to 8 servings

Double Baked Green Soybeans and Bacon

6 or 8 slices bacon
1/2 tsp. salt
1/4 tsp. pepper
2 Tbs. minced onion
2 c. cooked soybeans (or canned)
2 1/2 c. thin white sauce (see recipe below)
1 c. melba toast or bread crumbs

Preheat oven to 350 degrees.
Cook the bacon until almost crisp. Break into small pieces. Add the bacon, salt, pepper, onion, and some of the bacon drippings to the cooked soybeans in a baking dish. Top the beans with the white sauce and melba toast crumbs (or bread crumbs). Bake for 20 to 25 minutes.

White Sauce
Use 4 tablespoons of bacon fat or margarine to make the cream sauce. Add 1 1/2 cups hot milk. Bring to a boil and add 2 tablespoons of flour dissolved in a little milk. Add to the hot milk and cook until thickened.
Yields 4 servings

Meat Loaf with TVP*

1 tsp TVP (heaping)
1 tsp. beef base
1 c. water
2 lbs. lean ground beef
2 eggs
1/2 tsp. salt
1/2 tsp. pepper

Preheat oven to 375 degrees.
Place TVP and beef base in 1 cup water for about 5 minutes to soak.
Combine and mix the ground beef, eggs, salt, and pepper. Mix in the soaked
TVP and beef base. Spread mix in a 9- by 5-inch greased loaf pan. Bake for
about 40 minutes. Serve it sliced and hot with brown or mushroom gravy.
Yields 6 to 7 servings
*TVP *Textured Vegetable Protein*

Soybean Chili Con Carne

1 c. sliced onions
1/4 c. diced green pepper
1/2 c. soybean oil (or margarine)
2 lbs. beef rump steak cut into cubes
3 c. boiling water
1 c. tomato juice
1 Tbs. chili powder
2 tsp. salt
2 Tbs. brown sugar
1/2 c. diced sautéed onions
1 (2 lb.) can green soybeans
1 c. water (if needed)

In a heavy skillet, cook one cup onions and pepper in oil until tender. Add
cubed beef and cook until brown. Add the next 7 ingredients and cook
slowly for 1 hour or more. Add water if mixture thickens. Before meat is
tender, taste and add more spice or salt if desired.
Yields about 7 cups

Vegetable Soybean Loaf

2 c. cooked soybeans (or canned soybeans)
1 c. carrots
1/2 c. celery
1 medium onion
1 medium tomato
1 crushed tomato
1 large egg
1 tsp. salt
1/3 tsp. pepper
1 c. dry toasted soybean bread crumbs (or whole wheat crumbs)
1 sliced tomato for garnish

Preheat oven to 350 degrees.
Chop fine the soybeans, carrots, celery, onion, and tomato in a food chopper or processor. Add crushed tomato, beaten egg, salt, pepper, and dry crumbs. Mix well. Place in well-greased 9- by 5-inch loaf pan and bake 40 minutes or until done. Serve with a slice of fresh tomato.
Yields 5 servings

Soybean Meatless Loaf

2 c. cooked soybeans (or canned soybeans)
1 small ground onion
1/2 c. dry toasted soybean bread crumbs (or whole wheat crumbs)
1 large egg, beaten
1 crushed tomato
1/3 tsp. salt
1/4 tsp. pepper
chopped parsley

Preheat oven to 350 degrees.
Grind or chop fine in food processor, soybeans, onion, and dry crumbs. Add beaten egg, crushed tomato, salt, and pepper. Mix well. Pour mixture into a 9- by 5-inch greased loaf pan and bake about 35 minutes. Serve with your favorite gravy and top with some chopped parsley.
Yields 4 servings

Soybean Mush

2 c. cooked soybeans (or canned soybeans)

Press cooked soybeans through a coarse sieve or chop fine in a food processor. This can be used in making soups, croquettes, and stuffing. When cold it can be used for sandwich filling by adding some chopped onion for flavor, and salad dressing to make it easier to spread. Very nice on toast.
Yields 2 cups

Soybean Milk

1 c. soybean flour
4 c. water

Mix soybean flour and water well with a wire whip. Let rest for 1 1/2 hours. Stir once or twice, then cook in double boiler for 20 minutes. Strain through a fine sieve or cheesecloth. There is also a soy milk powder available on the market. Use 2 1/2 to 3 ounces of soy milk powder to 4 cups cold water. Stir well. You may add a teaspoon of honey or corn syrup and a pinch of salt. Do not hesitate to use this soy milk in any recipe in place of regular milk.
Yields 5 cups

Homemade Soybean Milk

1 c. soybeans
7 c. water

Soak clean, dry soybeans overnight in cold water. The next day, drain off, but save the water. Put the soybeans through the fine blade of a food processor, then add the ground beans to reserved water and bring to a boil. Reduce heat and simmer for 15 minutes. Strain mixture through a fine-meshed sieve or cheesecloth. Soybean milk may be flavored with a little honey.

This is especially good for people allergic to dairy products. It is wholesome, tasteful, and only a little lower in calcium than cow's milk.
Yields 7 cups

Roasted Soybeans

1 c. clean soybeans
1 tsp. salt
4 c. cold water

Preheat oven to 350 degrees.
Add soybeans and salt to water and let soak overnight. The next day boil the beans in the same water for 1 hour. Drain off the water and spread the soybeans on a shallow pan and roast them for 30 minutes. Be sure to have the vent fan operating to minimize a somewhat burned roasting aroma. Shake the pan several times to allow all the beans to turn light brown. Sprinkle with a little salt for taste.
   Roasted soybeans, when chopped or ground in a food mill, are used in decorating cakes, topping for puddings, salads, cookies, cakes, and ice cream. Store roasted soybeans in sealed jars for later use.
Yields 1 1/2 cups

Homemade Soybean Coffee
(No Caffeine)

3 c. clean soybeans

Place soybeans in a skillet or baking dish. Bake in a preheated 400 degree oven, stirring frequently until beans are dark brown (not black). Then grind them in a coffee grinder, as you would regular coffee (not too fine). Tastes nutty and similar to regular coffee, but no caffeine.
Yields 5 cups

The Clinton Inn (pictured) was the first building Henry Ford acquired for Greenfield Village in 1927. It was originally located in Clinton, Michigan, a stagecoach stop on the Chicago Road. At Greenfield Village I helped the management make over the kitchen of the inn to serve visitors cafeteria style. Presently the building is known as Eagle Tavern. Photograph courtesy of the Dearborn Historical Museum

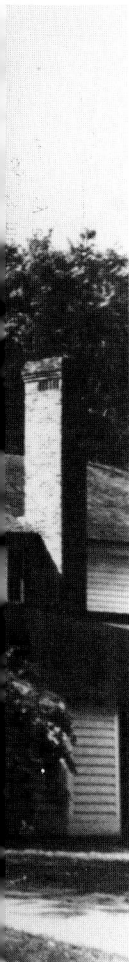

Part III
I Help Open the Clinton Inn Restaurant to the Public

When the old gentleman was no longer active, I left the company. I had decided to start a catering business on my own. So I had a building constructed on Telegraph Road south of Michigan Avenue and called my business Jan's Catering.

Soon some men from Greenfield Village came along and asked if they could bring Village visitors to my place to eat and hear about Henry Ford and his interest in soybeans. The Village was not serving anyone except employees and school children in those days.

I told them that I didn't have that much room. What they should do, I suggested, was serve the visitors right there at the historic Clinton Inn. The fellows agreed it was a good idea—if I helped them get started.

So I went there and helped change over the kitchen to cafeteria style. Only the Village school children had lunched there before. Now the public could come during the summer when school was out. It was up to me to arrange menus. No one said "do this" or "do that." The food was plain and very reasonably priced that first summer. But we did not have enough kitchen help. When Annie's family came from Boston to see us, I put them all to work in the cafeteria.

We served mostly chicken dinners, sandwiches, and soup. I was working seven days a week that summer and didn't have time for anything else. So I sold my catering business to some printers.

After the Fords died there weren't too many people around who knew about them. The manager of Fair Lane Estate would contact me when he had important guests from Europe or South America. He wanted me to come and talk about Mr. Ford and soybeans. I always brought samples so the visitors could taste the soybean products and see what they looked like.

I didn't go back to the Clinton Inn the next summer because management was provided by the village administration. Instead, I got a job as chef at the Garden City Hospital (when it was in Ypsilanti). We bought food from Miesel/Sysco wholesalers, and a couple of the salesmen were friendly. One gentleman was going to retire and asked, "Would you like to be one of our salesmen?"

I liked the way he dressed, and I said "yes." Well, I got the job and had it for thirty-two years. My title became Executive Chef, and as before, I was still called upon often to talk about Henry Ford and his interest in soybeans.

I lost my wife, Annie, in 1988. Two of my sons, Gerrit and Neil, have retired from Ford Motor Company—Neil, as a tool and die control analyst in 1991, and Gerrit, as senior programming and supply analyst in 1992. My youngest son, John, is the only one to follow in my footsteps and he is still employed as director of food services at the Beverly Hills Medical Center in Los Angeles, California. I have eight grandchildren and seven great-grand-children. As far as I know, there are no future chefs among them.

During the thirty years I worked for Mr. Ford I met many important and famous people. Sometimes I'm asked if any of them especially impressed me.

One who did was Dr. George Washington Carver, the botanical chemist. He was such a brilliant fellow, and I admired him for coming up from slavery and working himself to a top position. He was the first black graduate of Iowa State University. Even when he became Director of Research at Tuskegee Institute, Dr. Carver remained a down-to-earth person. He often ate in the dining room of Dearborn Inn with other VIPs, but sometimes he'd come into the kitchen to snack with me.

I admired Mrs. Ford, who was a motherly woman, and Edsel, who was pleasant and easy to please. But Edsel ate things he shouldn't have, considering his poor health.

Of all the people I met, the prince of them all was Mr. Henry Ford. He was a wonderful man. He was so interested in everything and everybody. He loved children. He helped them, and the poor, too, whenever he could.

Of course, I thought a lot of Dr. Ruddiman. He told me many times that you are what you eat. (What you eat today will walk and talk with you tomorrow.) Well, I've eaten soybean foods ever since I started experimenting with them. They must have been good for me. When my ninetieth birthday came around I was still working every day, driving my own car, and taking care of my own home and yard. I'm hardly ever sick.

It used to be everyone thought soybeans were just food for animals. Mr. Ford helped people realize that they are perfect food for human beings. He once said that, next to the Model T, he considered his soybean research to be his greatest work. I am thankful that because of that little bean I had such a pleasant association with this great man for so many years.

Soup
General Information

Soup has a twofold purpose: first to stimulate the appetite and second to provide nourishment. One should give special attention and consideration to this phase of cookery, because to become a master of the soup pot is a top office. Generally speaking, soup recipes are classified into three groups:

1. Thin, clear soups such as consommé, bouillon, and broth
2. Light cream soups such as cream of tomato, asparagus, celery, mushroom, pea, etc.
3. Thick soups such as chowder, bisque, pepper pot, scotch broth, mulligatawny, vegetable, etc.

A fourth soup category might be added—jellied consommé or cold vichyssoise, which are refreshing cold soups, usually served on hot summer days.

Here, members of my wife Annie's family help out in the kitchen of Clinton Inn. I recruited the Werner family when they came from Boston to visit me. The cashier is Marjorie Williams. Photograph courtesy of Jan Willemse

Soup's On!

Bean Soup

2 lb. dried northern beans
1 gal. cold water
2 qts. hot water
5 oz. ham flavored soup base

Wash beans well. Combine beans and cold water. Bring to a boil for 2 minutes. Remove from heat and let stand for 2 hours. Stir in hot water and ham base. Heat to boiling. Reduce heat and gently boil for 2 hours, until beans are tender. Remove and set aside 3 cups of cooked, drained beans. Purée the remaining soup and measure the yield. Add hot water, to make 3 quarts plus 1 cup. If more than desired quantity, simmer a little longer. Combine soup with the reserved cooked beans, mixing well. Heat and serve. You may add some diced cooked ham or some diced carrots for color.
Yields 21 6-ounce portions

French Onion Soup

1/2 c. butter (or soybean margarine)
4 c. sliced onions (1/8 inch thick and 1 inch long)
7 c. hot water
1 oz. beef base (or beef extract)
salt and pepper to taste

Melt butter in heavy saucepan or skillet. Slowly add onions and sauté until onions are tender and golden rich brown (approximately 8 to 10 minutes), being careful not to burn. Drain any extra fat. Add hot water, beef base, salt, and pepper to taste. Mix well. Heat to boiling point. Reduce heat and simmer 5 to 10 minutes. Serve hot, garnished with toasted Parmesan cheese croutons or crackers.
Yields 8 servings

Duchess Soup

3/4 c. carrots chopped or grated
3/4 c. finely diced celery
2 c. boiling water
3 Tbs. finely chopped onions
1/3 c. butter (or margarine)
1/3 c. flour
3 c. milk
3 c. chicken stock (or 3 cups water mixed with 2 tsp. chicken base)
12 oz. diced sharp American cheese
parsley, chopped

Simmer carrots and celery in lightly salted boiling water for 10 to 12 minutes. Sauté onions in butter until soft, but not brown. Add flour and blend well. Place over hot water and add milk and chicken stock. Cook until thickened, stirring constantly. Add cheese and stir until blended. Add cooked vegetables and their liquid and heat thoroughly. Serve topped with parsley and accompanied with melba toast, crackers, or bread sticks.
Yields 7 to 10 portions

Potato Soup

4 c. hot water
1 heaping tsp. chicken base
1/2 c. fresh, diced leeks
1/2 c. finely diced onions
3 c. clean (with skin on) diced potatoes
1 tsp. salt
1/2 tsp. pepper
1 c. cream (or canned evaporated milk)
chopped chives or parsley

Blend hot water, chicken base, leeks, onion, and potatoes. Add salt and pepper. Cook until potatoes are done. Finally, add the cream (or canned milk) and garnish with parsley or chives. Serve with a cracker or melba toast.
Yields 7 or 8 servings

Potato and Leek Soup

1 lb. peeled, sliced thin potatoes
2 c. finely diced onions
1/4 lb. white part of leeks, washed and sliced thin
7 c. hot chicken stock (or 7 c. hot water with 2 tsp. chicken base)
1/2 c. chopped clean parsley

Combine all ingredients, except parsley, and bring to a boil. Reduce heat and let simmer for 25 minutes or until ingredients are soft. Purée and season to taste. Sprinkle each serving with chopped parsley. Consistency may be adjusted with a small amount of cornstarch.
Yields 8 to 10 servings

Combination Pea Soup Quikee

1 can green peas
1 can evaporated milk
2 c. soybean milk (or regular milk)
1/2 tsp. salt
1/3 tsp. pepper

Purée undrained green peas. Add the milk, salt, and pepper. Heat and serve with soybean bread, croutons, or soybean bread toasted.
Yields 6 or 7 servings

Fresh Green Pea Soup

1 c. medium diced onions
1/4 c. soybean or vegetable oil
1/3 c. flour
7 c. hot water
1 heaping Tbs. chicken base
1 lb. frozen peas (or 1 lb. can green peas)

Sauté onions in oil in a heavy pan until tender but not brown. Add the flour and blend well. Cook and stir for 3 or 4 minutes without browning. Add chicken base to hot water and add four cups of the chicken stock to onion mixture. Cook until thickened. Purée peas and add to thickened chicken stock. Serve with melba toast or crackers.
Yields 8 to 10 servings

Quick Manhattan Clam Chowder

1/4 c. finely diced onions
1/2 c. finely diced celery
1/2 c. diced green pepper
2 c. small diced potato
5 c. boiling water
1 Tbs. clam base (can be found at gourmet food stores)
2 cups crushed, stewed tomatoes
1 8 oz. can chopped clams
salt and pepper to taste

Mix all ingredients in a heavy pot. Bring to a boil, lower the heat, and simmer for 5 minutes. Serve with melba toast, crackers, or croutons.
Yields 8 8-ounce servings

Rich Clam Bisque

1/3 c. margarine
3 Tbs. flour
2 cups hot milk
1 Tbs. clam base (can be found at gourmet food stores)
2 cups hot coffee cream (or canned, evaporated milk)
salt and pepper to taste

Melt margarine over low heat and blend in the flour with a wooden spoon or whip for 2 minutes, being careful not to brown. Add 2 cups hot milk and clam base. Heat to boiling and let simmer 5 to 8 minutes. Add 2 cups hot cream (or canned milk). Salt and pepper to taste. Serve with melba toast or wheat crackers.
Yields 4 to 5 servings

Grandma's Vegetable Soup

1 medium chopped onion
4 large carrots chopped
1 lb. potatoes scrubbed and chopped
3 stalks celery diced
6 c. chicken stock (or 6 c. hot water with 2 Tbs. chicken base)
1/4 tsp. salt
2 bay leaves
1/4 c. chopped parsley
1 1/2 c. grated Cheddar cheese

In a large, heavy saucepan or Dutch oven, combine vegetables and cover with stock and spices. Bring to a boil and simmer for 30 to 35 minutes or until vegetables are tender. Remove the bay leaves and serve hot topped with grated cheese.
Yields 6 to 7 servings

Beef Vegetable Soup

1 lb. ground beef
2 Tbs. vegetable oil
4 c. hot water
1 1/2 c. diced potatoes
1 c. small diced carrots
1 c. small diced onions
2 c. diced tomatoes
1 bay leaf
1 Tbs. salt
1/2 Tbs. pepper
1 Tbs. beef extract

Brown the ground beef in hot vegetable oil for about 10 minutes. Place browned beef in large pot. Add the hot water and all the other ingredients. Bring to a boil and let simmer until the vegetables are tender, but not mushy. Remove bay leaf. Serve with melba toast or crackers.
Yields 10 portions

Lentil Spinach Soup

2 Tbs. soybean (or olive) oil
1 large onion diced
8 c. water
3 Tbs. chicken base
1 lb. lentils, rinsed and drained
1 10 oz. package frozen spinach (defrosted and squeezed dry)
1/2 tsp. black pepper
1/8 tsp. allspice
1 tsp. salt
5 oz. shredded mozzarella cheese

In a large pot heat oil over medium heat. Add diced onions and sauté until golden brown, (about 3 minutes). Add water, chicken base, and lentils. Bring to a boil, reduce heat, and cover. Simmer for about 30 to 45 minutes until lentils are tender, stirring occasionally. Stir in spinach, spices, and salt. Simmer, covered for 15 minutes. Garnish with grated cheese and serve with melba toast or crackers.
Yields 10 to 12 portions

Cream of Asparagus Soup

5 c. chicken stock (or 5 c. boiling water with 2 heaping Tbs. of chicken base)
1 (17-oz.) can asparagus pieces
1 c. medium diced onions
1/3 of a bay leaf
2 oz. butter
1/3 c. flour
2 c. hot milk
1 c. hot light cream (or evaporated milk)
salt
pepper

Bring chicken stock to a boil. Add asparagus, onion, and bay leaf and simmer for 20 minutes. While simmering, melt butter and add flour to make a roux. Cook, stirring constantly, for 5 minutes over low heat (do not brown). Add stock to roux slowly until thickened and smooth. Bring to a boil. Heat milk and cream together and combine with thickened base. Adjust seasoning and keep warm.

Variations: Substitute three cups of carrots, cauliflower, or onion in place of the asparagus to make a variety of different cream soups.
Yields 10 portions

Cream of Broccoli Soup

5 c. chicken stock (or 5 cups boiling water with 1 Tbs. chicken base)
8 oz. fresh broccoli (or frozen)
1/4 c. diced onion
1/3 of a bay leaf
1/4 c. flour
2 oz. butter
2 c. milk, heated
3/4 c. light cream, heated
salt
pepper

Heat stock, broccoli, onions, and bay leaf and simmer for 10 to 20 minutes. Combine flour and butter to make the roux and cook, stirring constantly, for 3 to 5 minutes. Add heated stock to roux gradually—stirring until it thickens. Add heated milk and cream. Adjust seasoning by adding salt and pepper to taste.
Yields 8 10-ounce portions

Cream of Vegetable Soup

2 c. hot water
1 Tbs. chicken base
1 c. frozen mixed vegetables
1/3 c. finely chopped onions
1/2 c. small diced carrots
1/2 c. small diced celery
1/4 c. soft butter (or margarine)
2 Tbs. flour
1 1/2 c. milk
1 c. coffee cream (or canned milk)
1 tsp. salt
1/8 tsp. pepper

Boil the water and add the chicken base and vegetables. Cook until almost tender. Melt the butter and add the flour to make a roux. Heat the milk and cream and add to the roux, stirring briskly until nice and smooth. Add to the vegetable mixture and simmer for a few minutes. Add salt and pepper to taste.
Yields 5 to 6 portions

Hotel Style Cream of Mushroom Soup

2 oz. butter (or margarine)
1/2 lb. fresh mushrooms (washed and chopped fine)
2 Tbs. chopped onion
1 Tbs. flour
1 qt. chicken broth (or 1 Tbs. chicken base added to 1 qt. of water)
1 c. coffee cream (or canned milk)
1/2 bay leaf
1/2 clove garlic
1/4 tsp. peppercorn
2 sprigs parsley
1/8 tsp. cayenne pepper (or nutmeg)
salt

Melt butter in thick-bottomed pot. Add mushrooms and onions and cook 5 minutes over direct heat. Stir constantly. Add flour and blend well. Add chicken broth, stirring with whip until well blended. Cook over medium heat, stirring occasionally, until the mix reaches proper consistency. Add cream. Season with a bouquet garni made by tying together in cheesecloth the bay leaf, garlic, peppercorns, and parsley. Add cayenne or nutmeg. Remove bouquet before serving. Serve soup hot with melba toast or croutons.
Yields 3 or 4 portions

Cream of Tomato Soup

1/3 c. soy or vegetable oil
1/3 c. flour
4 c. hot water
1 Tbs. beef base
4 c. tomato purée
1 c. diced carrots
1 c. small diced celery
3/4 c. diced onions
1/2 Tbs. pepper
dash of garlic and clove
2 c. light cream (or milk)
salt

Heat oil. Add flour and blend well. Cook for 2 to 3 minutes. Add water and beef base. Add tomato purée, vegetables, and spices and simmer 20 to 40 minutes. Blend in light cream (or milk) and salt to taste.
Yields 7 to 10 portions

Cream of Chicken Soup

1/4 c. butter (or margarine)
1/3 c. flour
5 c. hot milk
4 c. diced chicken
1 c. cooked rice
1 tsp. celery salt
chopped parsley

Melt butter and blend in flour to form a roux. Add 5 cups of hot milk slowly. Keep stirring and let it come to a boil. Add the diced chicken, cooked rice, and celery salt. Let simmer for a while. Garnish with some chopped parsley. Serve hot with croutons or melba toast.
Yields 8 to 10 servings

Tomato Soup

1 Tbs. soybean or olive oil
1 small onion diced
4 green onions diced, including tops
2 Tbs. flour
4 c. hot chicken broth (or 4 cups boiling water with 1 heaping
Tbs. chicken base)
3 ripe tomatoes diced
1/2 tsp. salt
2 tsp. sugar
1/2 tsp. pepper
2 Tbs. chopped parsley

In a large saucepan heat oil over medium heat. Add onions and sauté for 2 or 3 minutes. Add flour and cook for 1 minute, stirring constantly. Pour into stock and heat to boiling. Add tomatoes, salt, sugar, pepper, and parsley. Reduce heat and simmer, covered, for 20 or 30 minutes or until the tomatoes are reduced to a pulp. Allow to cool. Then purée in a blender or processor. Reheat and serve with melba toast or whole wheat crackers.
Yields 6 servings

Jellied Tomato Soup

3 lb. peeled tomatoes chopped fine
4 c. chopped celery
2 c. chopped onion
Beef stock made with 4 cups hot water and 4 beef cubes
2 Tbs. sugar
1 tsp. salt
1/2 tsp. ground cloves
1/2 tsp. pepper
1 1/2 oz. unflavored gelatin
1/3 c. lemon juice

Simmer tomatoes, celery, onions, and stock for 15 minutes. Add sugar, salt, cloves, and pepper and simmer for another 15 minutes. Soak gelatin in small amount of water. Remove soup from heat. Stir in gelatin until dissolved. Add lemon juice and adjust seasonings. Strain and chill. Cut into cubes and serve in chilled cups.
Yields 8 9-ounce servings

Note: *Refrigerate a small amount of soup in sauce dish to test consistency before chilling entire amount. Gelatin often varies in power. Adjust if necessary. Add a small amount of red and yellow coloring if desired.*

The dining room of Fair Lane mansion was paneled in rose leaf mahogany wood. The room has been completely restored in recent years. Photograph courtesy of the University of Michigan-Dearborn

S A L A D S

Chef Salad Bowl

1 c. cooked chicken sliced in thin strips
1 c. cooked ham sliced in thin strips
2 c. sharp Cheddar cheese sliced in thin strips
3 hard-boiled eggs
salt and pepper
Thousand Island or French dressing

Toss meat and cheese together and place in lettuce-lined salad bowl that has been rubbed with garlic or onion. Garnish with hard-boiled egg slices. Sprinkle with salt and pepper. Serve with Thousand Island dressing or French dressing.
Yields 5 or 6 portions

Fresh Green Salad

1 small head lettuce
1/2 head endive
1/2 lb. spinach
1/2 tsp. salt
3/4 c. French dressing
2 hard-boiled eggs
grated cheese

Wash all greens. Break into bite-size pieces. Place in a round bowl, add French dressing, and toss greens to coat. Refrigerate salad. Serve 1-cup portions in a salad bowl on leaf lettuce. Top with some grated cheese and one slice of hard-boiled egg.
Yields 10 portions

Sprout Combination Salad

1 pt. small, slightly cooked sprouts
1 c. diced celery
6 to 8 thinly sliced radishes
1 medium sliced or diced cucumber
1 head shredded lettuce
1/8 tsp. salt
6–8 lettuce leaves
6–8 pepper rings
French or soybean salad dressing

Mix first 6 ingredients, cover with a damp cloth, and refrigerate. Serve on leaf lettuce. Top with a thin slice of pepper ring and French or soybean salad dressing.
Yields 6 to 8 portions

Cabbage and Pineapple Salad

6 c. shredded cabbage
1 c. pineapple tidbits
4 oz. small mushrooms, sliced
1/2 tsp. salt
1 c. mayonnaise or salad dressing
1 head lettuce, broken into bite-size pieces

Lightly mix or toss ingredients.
Yields 8 portions

Low Calorie Fruit Salad

1 lb. grapes
1 grapefruit sectioned
2 oranges sectioned
3 large apples diced (dipped in lemon juice)
1/2 c. diced celery
1/2 c. low fat salad dressing
8 lettuce leaves
3/4 c. chopped salted soybeans (or peanuts)

Mix fruit, celery, and salad dressing. Place one scoop of mixture on lettuce leaf. Top with 1 tablespoon roasted soybeans (or peanuts).
Yields 8 portions

Molded Lime Fruit Salad

4 oz. package lime gelatin
2 c. boiling water
1 25 1/2 oz. can pear halves, drained. Reserve juice
1 25 1/2 oz. can sliced pineapple, drained. Reserve juice
1/2 c. lemon juice and some grated lemon rind
1 large head lettuce

Dissolve gelatin in boiling water. Add pear, pineapple, lemon juice and rind to gelatin mixture. Place a pear half and half slice of pineapple in each mold, or all in a large dish. Cover with gelatin mixture and allow to set in refrigerator at least 2 hours or overnight. Unmold on lettuce just before serving and refrigerate until service begins. Serve with mayonnaise, cooked dressing, or fruit salad dressing. (See salad dressings.)
Yields 10 portions

Orange Date Salad

6 peeled oranges
1/2 lb. small pitted dates
1/3 c. sugar
1/2 c. chopped pecans
1 large head lettuce (or leaf lettuce)
Fruit dressing or whipped cream

Slice oranges. Roll dates in sugar. Place 10 sections of orange and four dates in each lettuce cup (or leaf). Sprinkle chopped pecans over each salad. Serve with fruit salad dressing or whipped cream.
Yields 10 portions

Stuffed Pear Salad

1/2 lb. softened cream cheese
1 c. crushed pineapple
1/2 c. chopped pecans
1/2 c. maraschino cherries
10 large pear halves
1 head lettuce shredded, or leaf lettuce

Beat the cream cheese. Mix crushed pineapple, chopped pecans, and chopped cherries. Place a small scoop of mixture in the center of a chilled pear half. Serve on shredded lettuce or leaf lettuce.
Yields 10 portions

Stuffed Peach Salad

1 c. walnuts or pecans
1 c. cleaned raisins
1/2 c. lemon juice
1 25 1/2 oz. can peach halves, chilled
1 head of lettuce, shredded, or leaf lettuce
salad dressing

Grind nuts and raisins together, add lemon juice and mix well. Chill. Place chilled peach halves on leaf or shredded head lettuce. Fill peach cavity with a small scoop of filling. Serve with salad dressing in a souffle cup on the side.
Yields 8 portions

Melon Salad

1 large cucumber partially peeled (leave some green for color)
1 cantaloupe with seeds removed
1 bunch radishes washed
1/4 c. wine vinegar
1/8 tsp. black pepper
4 to 6 leaves of lettuce, rinsed and dried

Cut cucumber into thin slices. Cut cantaloupe into cubes or small melon balls. Slice radishes thin. Combine all ingredients in a bowl and toss with wine vinegar. Sprinkle with black pepper. Serve chilled on plates lined with lettuce leaves.
Yields 5 portions

Grandma-Style Potato Salad

2 lb. washed potatoes with skins on
3 young green onions with tops
   (chopped)
1 red or green bell pepper (cleaned
   and chopped)
5 radishes sliced
3 washed celery ribs chopped finely
1/3 c. finely chopped parsley
paprika

Dressing
1 c. mayonnaise
1/3 c. cider (or wine) vinegar
1/2 tsp. ground pepper
1 tsp. salt
1 tsp. prepared mustard
1 tsp. celery seed
1 Tbs. chopped dill weed

Boil potatoes until tender. When cool, cut potatoes into half-inch cubes and put into a large bowl. Combine potatoes with onions, peppers, radishes, chopped celery, and chopped parsley. Mix together dressing ingredients and add to the diced potato mixture. Sprinkle with chopped parsley and dust with paprika. Chill for at least two hours or longer.
Yields 10 portions

Chicken Fruit Salad

3 c. diced cooked chicken
1 10 oz. can mandarin oranges, drained
1 10 oz. can pineapple tidbits, drained
1 c. sliced grapes
1 c. finely diced celery
2 Tbs. vinegar
3 Tbs. orange juice
1 tsp. salt
1/3 c. mayonnaise
1/3 c. toasted slivered almonds (or chopped pecans)

Combine chicken, oranges, pineapple tidbits, grapes, and celery. Combine the remaining ingredients (except almonds) and add to fruit and chicken. Just before serving add the toasted almonds (or chopped pecans).
Yields 8 to 10 portions

Grandma's Chicken Salad

2 c. diced cooked chicken
1 c. finely diced celery
1 Tbs. fine diced onion
1/4 c. lemon juice
1 c. mayonnaise
1/4 c. toasted slivered almonds (or chopped pecans)
1/2 tsp. salt
1 tsp. nutmeg
2 sliced hard-boiled eggs.

Combine chicken, celery, onion, and lemon juice. Let chill for 10 minutes in refrigerator. Mix mayonnaise, almonds, salt, and nutmeg. Add to chicken mixture. Garnish with sliced eggs and sprinkle with chopped parsley.
Yields 6 portions

Turkey or Chicken Salad

1/2 lb. cut up leftover chicken or turkey
1 lb. romaine lettuce or spinach, torn in bite-size pieces
1/2 green or red pepper sliced thin
1 c. sliced black olives
1 1/2 c. mayonnaise
1/2 c. grated cheese
4 to 5 thin tomato slices

In a large bowl combine chicken, cleaned lettuce (or spinach), sliced pepper, black olives, and mayonnaise. Mix well. Top with grated cheese and a thin slice of tomato.
 Yields 4 or 5 portions

Tuna Salad Sandwich Spread
(for large parties)

1 (4 lb.) can tuna fish
3 oz. light TVP (textured vegetable protein)
2 to 3 c. mayonnaise
2 c. finely chopped celery (or 1 c. finely chopped onion)

Drain tuna, reserving liquid. Add three ounces of TVP to the tuna liquid. Let stand for 10 minutes, then mix or blend into drained and flaked tuna. Add 2 to 3 cups mayonnaise (or salad dressing). Add celery. You may substitute onion, or combine celery and onion for variety.
Yields 35 to 40 sandwiches

Tuna Egg Salad

1 (7 oz.) can tuna
2 Tbs. finely chopped onion
1/2 c. mayonnaise (or salad dressing)
1 tsp. lemon juice
1/2 tsp. salt
1/2 tsp. marjoram
1/8 tsp. white pepper
3 hard-boiled eggs, chopped, reserving 3 to 4 slices for garnish
3-4 lettuce leaves
1/2 tsp. paprika

Open tuna fish and empty, undrained, in a mixing bowl. Add the onion, mayonnaise (or salad dressing), lemon juice, salt, marjoram, pepper, and chopped eggs. Mix well. Serve on lettuce leaves, garnished with a thin slice of hard-boiled egg and dusted with a little paprika.
Yields 3 or 4 portions

Snappy Fruit Dressing

1 tsp. salt
3 Tbs. sugar
1 tsp. dry mustard (or prepared mustard)
1/4 c. lemon juice
1/8 c. orange juice
1 c. corn (or soybean oil)

Mix dry ingredients. Add enough lemon juice to make a thin paste. Using the mixer at low speed, add slowly, alternating fruit juice and oil, until the mixture becomes somewhat heavy. Alternate the remaining oil and fruit juice slowly until all is blended.
Yields 1/2 cups dressing

Clear French Dressing

1 tsp. dry or prepared mustard
1 Tbs. salt
3 Tbs. sugar
1 Tbs. onion juice
1/4 c. white vinegar
2 c. soybean oil

Mix and blend mustard, salt, sugar, onion juice, and vinegar. Add oil gradually, beating constantly.
Yields 1 pint dressing

Creamy Herb Dressing

1 c. mayonnaise
1/2 c. sour cream
1 Tbs. chopped parsley
1 Tbs. finely chopped onion
1 Tbs. chopped chives
1 tsp. anchovy paste
1 tsp. garlic or onion juice

Combine all ingredients and mix well. Chill. Stir before serving.
Yields 8 2-ounce servings

Green Goddess Dressing

1/2 c. chopped parsley
1/2 c. chopped watercress
3 Tbs. tarragon vinegar
2 Tbs. anchovy paste
2 Tbs. chopped chives
2 Tbs. corn or soy oil

Combine parsley, watercress, vinegar, anchovy paste, and chives. Place in blender at high speed for 1 minute. Keeps well in the refrigerator.
Yields 5 servings

Blue Cheese French Dressing

1 tsp. salt
1 tsp. pepper
1 Tbs. dry mustard
1 Tbs. fine minced onion
1/2 c. vinegar
1/2 c. blue cheese crumbled
1 c. corn (or soybean) oil

Mix dry ingredients. Add onion and vinegar and blend well. Add oil slowly while beating. Just before serving add the crumbled blue cheese.
Yields 1 pint dressing

Honey Ranch Dressing

1 c. soybean oil
1 c. ketchup
1 c. pure lemon juice
1 c. honey
1/2 tsp. salt
1 tsp. paprika

Mix thoroughly to blend well. Can be used on fruit salads or vegetable salads.
Yields 4 cups dressing

Honey Herb Dressing

2 c. low fat sour cream (or sour milk)
1/2 tsp. salt
1/2 tsp. Cajun mixed spice (optional)
1/3 c. honey (or brown sugar)
3 Tbs. mayonnaise
4 green onions with tops minced
1/3 c. chopped parsley

Using a hand or machine beater, whip together sour cream (or sour milk), salt, spice, honey, and mayonnaise. Stir in the remaining ingredients. Keeps well for weeks when refrigerated.
Yields 3 cups dressing

Chiffonade Dressing

1 c. white vinegar
1 c. corn (or soybean) oil
1/2 c. sugar
1 Tbs. salt
1 Tbs. dry mustard
2 Tbs. finely chopped onions
1/4 c. finely chopped green peppers
1/4 c. finely chopped pimiento
1 large finely chopped hard-boiled egg

Mix the vinegar, oil, sugar, salt, and mustard. Just before serving add chopped onions, pepper, pimiento, and egg.
Yields 3 cups dressing

The beautiful ballroom at Lovett Hall in Greenfield Village had
its own stage where musicians played for Early American dances
hosted every week by the Fords. There were also a fireplace and
three sparkling chandeliers of crystal. The ballroom looks much
the same today. However, it is used mostly now for luncheons
and dinners as this recent photograph shows. Photograph
courtesy of the Henry Ford Museum and Greenfield Village

Finger Foods

Suggestions for Leftover Turkey
Could be used to make a turkey salad, or the well-known turkey club sandwich, or you can grind leftover turkey pieces into a smooth sandwich paste filling mixed with mayonnaise or salad dressing. Another idea would be to make a turkey pot pie. For the pie, in an individual baking dish, put diced turkey and cream of chicken soup, a piecrust top, or top with mashed potatoes. Add a sprinkle of paprika before baking in an oven at 350 degrees.

Ham and Cheese Sandwich

2 slices bread (or multigrain bun)
1 Tbs. tartar sauce
2 oz. thin sliced (shaved) ham
2 slices Cheddar (or Swiss) cheese
sliced lemon (or parsley)

Toast sliced bun (or bread slices). Spread with tartar sauce, then add layer of ham and a slice of cheese, then another slice of ham. Top with remaining bun (or slice of bread) and cut diagonally. Garnish with a slice of lemon (or sprig of parsley).
Yields 1 sandwich

Roast Beef Sandwich

2 sliced hamburger buns (or 4 slices multigrain bread)
3 Tbs. tartar sauce (or your favorite condiment)
2 leaf lettuce (or shredded lettuce)
2 oz. roast beef sliced very thin (shaved)
Sliced tomato, bean sprouts and/or onion slices

Toast sliced buns (or slices of bread). Spread with tartar sauce (or your favorite condiment), then add lettuce and roast beef. Close sandwich with top of bun (or another slice of bread) and fasten together with a frill pick. For additional flavoring add sliced tomato, bean sprouts, or even a thin slice of fresh onion.
Yields 2 sandwiches

Finger Sandwiches for Parties

You can create a great variety of finger sandwiches by using different fillings. Use peanut butter and any number of different jellies or jams, a variety of luncheon meats and cheeses. These sandwiches can be cut in endless shapes and sizes.

After sandwiches are prepared and cut into desired shapes, place them on serving trays. Cover them with a clean damp towel and place them in the refrigerator until you need them. Garnish with a slice of lemon or a sprig of parsley.

Creamy Lobster Dip

1 lb. softened cream cheese
1 c. sour cream
1 c. mayonnaise
4 tsp. lemon juice
3 Tbs. lobster base (available at gourmet food stores)
1 tsp. parsley

Blend cream cheese, sour cream, and mayonnaise thoroughly. Add lemon juice and lobster base. Mix well. Sprinkle with parsley and chill in refrigerator.
Serves at least 25

Chicken Sandwiches

1 baked chicken (legs and breast)
1/3 c. soft butter (or melted margarine)
1 Tbs. chopped chives (or parsley)
1/4 tsp. salt
1/4 tsp. pepper
1/3 c. soft butter (or melted margarine)
10 slices white bread (or whole wheat)

Remove chicken from the bone and discard the skin. Place the meat and 1/3 cup butter in a food processor and chop into a smooth paste. Season with chives (or parsley), salt, and pepper. Spread remaining 1/3 cup butter on the bread. Place the chicken paste on one side of the bread and cover with another slice of bread. Trim the crust. Cut into finger, round, half-moon, or diamond shapes. Cover sandwiches with a clean damp napkin and refrigerate until serving time.
Yields 5 sandwiches

Mrs. Henry Ford is pictured at the entrance of her prize English garden at her home, Fair Lane, in May of 1939. The wrought-iron gates were brought from England by Mr. Ford as a gift to Clara. Photograph courtesy of the University of Michigan-Dearborn

Part IV
How You Can Be As Healthy As Mr. Ford

Clara Ford loved flowers. She had many beautiful gardens at Fair Lane Estate that people came from all over the United States to see. One garden that was useful, as well as pretty, was her herb garden, which was close to the mansion. In it were herbs such as chives, parsley, rosemary, basil, and mints. And there was lavender, too, to add perfume and color.

Mrs. Ford asked the family cook, Maria, to use herbs in cooking at the mansion, particularly when she had invited lady friends to lunch.

Henry Ford, on the other hand, did not like many seasonings. When I cooked for him I hardly ever used herbs or spices and very little salt and pepper. Sometimes when he'd come into the kitchen and see the spices all lined up on the shelves he'd pretend to be angry and jokingly tell me to get rid of them, or else get rid of the cooks. He declared that spices were bad for the kidneys. They go through the body by way of the kidneys, he'd say.

But he allowed me to use small amounts of salt and pepper and occasionally herbs. The old gentleman was ahead of his time in recognizing that too much salt could raise blood pressure.

My guidelines for Americans who would like to be as healthy as Mr. Ford are to cut down as well on saturated fat and cholesterol. Choose lean meats, fish, poultry, and peas and dried beans of all kinds, including soybeans. Beans are a high source of protein.

Use skim or low-fat milk and dairy products and a moderate amount of egg yolks and organ meats. Broil, bake, or boil rather than fry. Trim fat from meats. In other words, limit your intake of fats.

Also, avoid too much sugar. Read food labels. If sugar, sucrose, glucose, maltose, dextrose, fructose, or syrup appear near the beginning of the ingredient list, the food contains a large amount of sugar. Select fresh fruits or fruits processed in their own juice or in light syrup.

While I was in Mr. Ford's employ we grew our own vegetables in the gardens at Greenfield Village. We knew they were always fresh. But with the large increase in population and long distances between food sources today it's difficult to get fresh produce unless you have your own garden. That's why I prefer frozen foods. They are picked, cleaned, and frozen right out of the gardens, and are fresher than the so-called fresh vegetables that must be sprayed with chemicals in order to look good on the counters of supermarkets.

Finally, if you want to feel young and full of pep do what your mama told you and eat your oatmeal every day. It can be cooked any style and served with a little honey or sugar, sprinkled with a little wheat germ or a teaspoon of TVP (soybean flakes) and/or raisins. Oatmeal is very rich in vitamin E and an excellent source of protein. In fact, like the soybean, it is almost a perfect food.

Eating oatmeal is an old custom. I have been in the habit of eating it for over sixty years. It did not do anything for my looks, but it gives me plenty of energy.

The pleasure of your company

is requested by

The Thomas Alva Edison Winter Home

Board of Directors

and

N C N B National Bank of Florida

at the Champagne Debut of

The Henry Ford Winter Home

Fort Myers, Florida

on Friday, the twenty-sixth of January

One thousand nine hundred and ninety

from five until seven o'clock in the evening

This invitation was sent to me to attend the opening of the Henry Ford Winter Home in Fort Myers, Florida, as a historical site. Though I was unable to attend, I sent some of my Model T crackers that were served with other favorite treats of the Fords at the affair. Photograph courtesy of Jan Willemse

Entrees

Pot Roast of Beef

5 lb. beef round (or chuck)
vegetable shortening
1 Tbs. salt
1/2 tsp. pepper
2 c. water

Heat Dutch oven. Add a little vegetable shortening and brown meat. Add salt and pepper. Add water. Simmer, covered, for 1 1/2 hours. Slice thin into 3-ounce portions. Top with a nice brown gravy. (See sauces and gravies.)
Yields 15 4-ounce portions

Swiss Steak

1 c. flour
1 tsp. salt
1/3 tsp. pepper
4 lb. beef round cut in 10 6-oz. pieces
1/2 c. vegetable shortening
1 1/2 c. water
5 c. brown gravy

Preheat oven to 350 degrees.
Mix flour, salt, and pepper. Dredge meat in mixture. Brown in shortening. Place in deep baking pan, add water, and cover. Bake for 45 minutes. Cover with gravy and bake for another 45 to 60 minutes.

Brown gravy
To 1/2 cup melted vegetable shortening, add 1/2 cup flour and stir. Cook for 5 minutes and remove from heat. Then add 4 cups hot water and 1 tablespoon beef base. Stir constantly until gravy thickens.
Yields 10 portions

Roulade of Beef

6 4-oz beef slices
3/4 lb. rich stuffing, like turkey dressing
1 qt. brown gravy

Preheat oven to 400 degrees.
Pound beef slices until very thin. Place one small scoop of stuffing on each slice of beef and roll it up. Place in greased pan. Brown meat lightly in oven for about 5 minutes. Add 4 cups of brown gravy and cover with aluminum foil. Simmer for 30 minutes at 350 degrees until nice and tender. Serve with brown gravy.

Brown gravy
To 1/2 cup melted vegetable shortening, add 1/2 cup flour and stir. Cook for 5 minutes and remove from heat. Then add 4 cups hot water and 1 tablespoon beef base. Stir constantly until gravy thickens.
Yields 6 portions

Swedish Meatballs

2 lb. ground beef
1 lb. ground pork
2 Tbs. chopped onions
3 eggs
3/4 c. milk
1 Tbs. salt
1 tsp. nutmeg
1/2 tsp. allspice
flour

Combine all ingredients except flour in mixer, using a flat paddle at low speed for one minute. Shape into 1-ounce balls. Roll balls in flour and brown in 350-degree hot fat. Place balls in baking pan and cover with brown gravy. Bake for 30 minutes in the oven at 325 degrees.

Brown gravy
To 1/2 cup melted vegetable shortening, add 1/2 cup flour and stir. Cook for 5 minutes and remove from heat. Then add 4 cups hot water and 1 tablespoon beef base. Stir constantly until gravy thickens.
Yields 12 to 15 portions

Meatballs with Barbecue Sauce

1 1/2 lb. ground beef (or hamburger)
1/2 lb. ground pork shoulder
1/2 c. milk (or water)
2 eggs
1 Tbs. salt
pinch pepper
1/3 c. finely chopped onion
barbecue sauce

Preheat oven to 300 degrees.
Mix meat well with milk (or water), eggs, salt, pepper, and onions. Shape into two-ounce meatballs and place close together in baking pan. Cover and bake until slightly brown. Pour off fat and cover with barbecue sauce. Bake meat covered for 30 to 35 minutes, and then bake 10 minutes uncovered for browning.
Yields 10 portions—two meatballs each

Savory Meatballs

2 lb. ground beef
1 (3 oz.) can evaporated milk
3 Tbs. chili sauce
1 Tbs. Worcestershire sauce
2 eggs
1 c. bread crumbs
1 tsp. salt
pinch black pepper

Preheat oven to 350 degrees.
Combine all ingredients and mix well for 2 minutes. Shape into 2-ounce meatballs and place in baking pan. Bake 30 to 35 minutes. Serve with a nice brown gravy.

Brown gravy
To 1/2 cup melted vegetable shortening, add 1/2 cup flour and stir. Cook for 5 minutes and remove from heat. Then add 4 cups hot water and 1 tablespoon beef base. Stir constantly until gravy thickens.
Yields 10 portions—2 meatballs each

Barbecued Beef on a Bun

2 lb. ground beef
1 c. chopped celery
2 Tbs. chopped onions
1 Tbs. vinegar
1 Tbs. Worcestershire sauce
2 tsp. salt
1/2 tsp. paprika
1/2 tsp. pepper
1/2 tsp. chili powder
1/2 c. water
1 1/2 c. ketchup
10 hamburger buns (sliced)

Brown ground beef. Sauté chopped celery and onions and combine with meat and remaining ingredients, except buns. Cook until meat is tender, about 20 to 25 minutes. Serve on plain or toasted buns or toasted bread.
Yields 10 3 1/2-ounce portions

Oven Barbecued Steak

10 6-oz. steaks
1/2 c. margarine
3/4 c. sliced onions
1 c. ketchup
3/4 c. vinegar
1/2 c. brown sugar
2 c. water
1 Tbs. dry or prepared mustard
1 Tbs. Worcestershire sauce
1 tsp. salt
1 tsp. pepper

Preheat oven to 350 degrees.
Brown steaks in margarine. Transfer to baking pans. Sauté onions in margarine after meat is removed. Mix remaining ingredients with the onions. Simmer and stir for 5 minutes. Add to steaks, making sure there is enough liquid to cover the meat. Cover and bake 45 minutes until tender.
Yields 10 6-ounce portions

Grandma's Marinated Steak

2 lb. flank steaks
1/2 tsp. black pepper

Marinade
3 Tbs. vegetable oil
3 Tbs. vinegar
3/4 c. red wine
1/2 tsp. garlic powder
1/2 tsp. oregano
1/2 tsp. salt
1/4 tsp. black pepper
1 bay leaf

Rub steaks with pepper. Combine all marinade ingredients and mix well. Pour over the steak. Refrigerate eight hours or overnight. Preheat the broiler. Remove steak from marinade and pat dry. Broil for approximately 7 to 10 minutes, or bake in 350-degree oven for 15 to 18 minutes.
Yields 6 to 7 servings

Beef à la Mode

2 lbs. lean beef round or rump
1 tsp. salt
1/2 tsp. pepper
1/4 c. roughly cut onions
1/4 c. roughly cut carrots
1/4 c. roughly cut celery
1/8 tsp. garlic
1/3 c. tomato paste
3 c. hot water mixed with 1 tsp. beef base

Preheat oven to 350 degrees.
Rub meat with salt and pepper. Brown meat in Dutch oven, turning often. Cover evenly with cut vegetables. Combine garlic, tomato paste, and beef stock. Pour over meat and cover tightly. Cook for about 1 hour to an internal temperature of 175 degrees (or until tender). Remove meat from oven, strain drippings. Separate broth to make gravy. Slice meat across the grain.
Yields 7 servings

Beef Vegetable Stew

3 lb. cubed round of beef
3/4 c. flour
1 Tbs. salt
1/2 tsp. pepper
1/2 c. shortening
3 c. hot water
1 bay leaf
1/2 tsp. allspice
1/2 c. chopped onions
Additional hot water if needed
3 c. diced carrots
3 c. diced potatoes
2 c. diced celery

Dredge meat in mixture of flour, salt, and pepper. Brown in hot shortening. Put meat in Dutch oven, add 3 cups of hot water, spices, and chopped onions. Cook slowly for 1 1/2 to 2 hours. Add additional hot water if needed. Boil carrots, potatoes, and celery for 15 to 20 minutes. Drain. Add to meat 30 minutes before serving. Continue cooking. If necessary, thicken with flour.
Yields 10 3/4-cup portions

Ground Beef Vegetable Stew

1 lb. coarse ground beef
1 c. sliced onions
2 c. hot water
1 Tbs. beef base
1 c. ketchup
1 Tbs. flour
1 Tbs. butter
1 Tbs. salt
1/4 tsp. pepper
1 (25 1/2 oz.) can drained mixed vegetables or peas, juice reserved
3 c. diced potatoes, boiled 10 minutes

Preheat oven to 350 degrees.
Sauté meat and onions. Heat water, beef base, ketchup, flour, butter, salt and pepper, and juice of mixed vegetables. Add to meat and onions. Bake covered, for 40 minutes. Add mixed vegetables and potatoes. Remove cover and bake for 15 minutes longer.
Yields 8 portions

Roast Tenderloin of Beef

2 lbs. beef tenderloin
1/4 c. melted shortening or oil
1/2 tsp. salt
1/4 tsp. pepper

Preheat oven to 400 degrees.
Place tenderloin on baking pan, folding narrow end under to make uniform thickness. Brush with melted shortening. Sprinkle with salt and pepper and insert meat thermometer into center of thickest part of fillet. Bake for 25 to 30 minutes for medium or rare (internal temperature 140 degrees). Remove from oven (keep warm) and slice straight across fibers. Serve as needed with mushroom gravy, or au jus may be served over dressing or rice pilaf. It may also be served with Bordelaise sauce.
Yields 6 to 8 servings

Swiss Steak Holland Style

10 (5 oz.) Delmonico or flank steaks
3/4 c. flour
1 tsp. salt
1/2 tsp. pepper
vegetable oil
1/2 c. chopped onions
1/2 c. chopped carrots
1/2 c. chopped celery
1 tsp. Worcestershire sauce
1 small can tomato sauce
1 tsp. beef base dissolved in 6 cups water

Preheat oven to 350 degrees.
Mix flour, salt, and pepper. Dredge steaks through seasoned flour. Brown on both sides in hot oil. Place steaks in deep roasting pan and top with chopped vegetables. Mix Worcestershire, tomato sauce, and beef stock. Add to beef and cover roasting pan. Bake for 1 1/2 hours until meat is tender. Take steaks out of roasting pan and keep warm. Strain the pan juices and put some back over the steaks. Use the rest as gravy.
Yields 10 portions

Meat Loaf

2 lb. lean ground beef
1 1/2 c. bread crumbs
3 Tbs. chopped onions
2 Tbs. chopped green peppers
1 Tbs. chopped parsley
2 eggs
1 tsp. salt
1/2 tsp. pepper
1 tsp. Worcestershire sauce
1 1/2 c. tomato purée

Preheat oven to 350 degrees.
Place first five ingredients in a mixer bowl. Mix in eggs, seasoning, and tomato purée. Mix well. Place in a 9- by 5-inch loaf pan. Bake for 1 hour.
Yields 10 to 12 servings

Rolled Round or Flank Steak with Dressing and Gravy

1 qt. hot water
2 tsp. sage
2 Tbs. salt
1 tsp. pepper
2/3 c. milk powder
1 c. margarine
2/3 c. chopped onion
2 lb. bread (soft cubes)
1 lb. diced celery
8 lb. beef round (or flank) sliced thin in 24 slices

Preheat oven to 350 degrees.
Combine water, seasoning, dry milk, margarine, and onion and add to bread cubes and celery. Place a scoop of dressing on each slice of meat. Roll meat around dressing. Place meat in deep baking pans and add 1/2 inch of water to each pan and cover pans. Cover and bake for 1 hour. Serve with 1 1/2 ounces of gravy. (See sauces and gravies.)
Yields 24 portions

Beef Burgundy

1/2 c. sliced onion
1/3 c. vegetable oil
1 lb. cubed beef
1/2 tsp. salt
1/8 tsp. black pepper
1/8 tsp. paprika
1/8 tsp. garlic
4 c. beef stock (or 4 c. water and beef base)
1/2 c. chopped mushrooms
1/2 c. chopped tomatoes
1/2 c. burgundy
chopped parsley

Preheat oven to 375 degrees.
Sauté onions in vegetable oil in a frying pan. Do not brown. Brown meat in same pan after the onions are removed. When the meat is somewhat brown, mix all ingredients, except the wine. Pour over meat and place in oven. Cover and bake until meat is tender. Just before serving, add the burgundy wine and serve over cooked rice. Garnish with some chopped parsley.
Yields 6 to 8 servings

Short Rib Jardiniere

5 lb. beef short ribs
1 c. reserved pan drippings
1 c. diced celery
1 c. diced onion
1 c. diced carrots
1/3 c. flour
1 Tbs. salt
1 tsp. pepper
1 crushed bay leaf
1 Tbs. beef base
1 qt. hot water
2 c. barbecue sauce

Preheat oven to 400 degrees.
Place ribs in single layers in baking pans. Bake for 25 to 30 minutes or until brown. Place ribs in a roasting pan. Reserve the pan drippings. Sprinkle diced vegetables over the browned ribs. Blend flour, salt, and pepper with 1 cup pan drippings in a saucepan. Dissolve beef base in a quart of hot water and stir into flour mixture with barbecue sauce. Cook and pour sauce over ribs and vegetables. Bake, covered, at 300 degrees until meat is tender.
Yields 8 to 10 portions.

Farm Style Chicken

1 c. diced celery
1 c. water
1 small diced onion
1/2 c. diced green pepper
1/3 c. diced pimiento
5 Tbs. butter
2 c. milk
2 c. mushroom soup
1/2 tsp. salt
6 c. diced cooked chicken
1 c. grated soft cheese
1 c. fine bread crumbs

Preheat oven to 375 degrees.
Cook celery in one cup of water for five minutes only, then drain off the water. Add the onion, green pepper, pimiento and butter and simmer slowly for a few minutes. Add the milk, mushroom soup, salt, and the diced chicken. Cook for about 5 to 10 minutes, stirring a few times. Pour into greased casserole. Mix grated cheese and bread crumbs and sprinkle on top and bake 30 minutes until golden brown.
Serves 10

Baked Chicken

4 chicken halves
1/2 c. all purpose flour
1 tsp. salt
1/3 tsp. pepper
1/2 c. melted butter
1 c. chopped onions

Preheat oven to 400 degrees.
Mix the flour, salt, and pepper. Brush the chicken with the melted butter and dredge the chicken with the spiced flour. Place the chicken in a well-greased casserole with some chopped onions and bake for about 25 minutes until golden brown. Reduce heat to 350 degrees and finish the chicken until nice and tender or well done.
Serves 4

Chicken or Turkey Croquettes

2 lb. mashed potatoes
2 whole eggs
3/4 lb. cooked chicken or turkey scraps, chopped fine
1 tsp. chicken base
1/4 c. milk
1 Tbs. chopped parsley
1/2 tsp. salt
1/2 tsp. nutmeg
1/2 tsp. pepper

Mix all ingredients until nice and smooth. Mold into 10 3-ounce croquettes.
Deep fry or bake in 375-degree oven. Serve 1 or 2 croquettes on a plate.
Garnish with cream or chicken gravy, mushroom gravy, or tomato sauce.
Yields 10 3-ounce portions

Chicken Casserole

3 c. diced cooked chicken
2 c. sliced small celery
1/2 c. sliced almonds
1/2 tsp. salt
1/2 tsp. white pepper
1 Tbs. grated onion
3 Tbs. lemon juice
1 c. mayonnaise
1/2 c. sour cream
2 c. crushed potato chips
1 c. shredded processed Cheddar-style cheese

Preheat oven to 375 degrees.

Mix first 9 ingredients. Fill an 8- by 10-inch baking dish. Mix together crushed potato chips and shredded cheese and sprinkle over the top. Bake for about 15 minutes.
Serves 7 to 8

Home-Style Creamed Chicken

4 c. diced cooked chicken
1 c. diced cooked potatoes
1 c. diced cooked carrots
1 c. canned green peas
1/4 c. canned pearl onions
4 c. cream sauce

Mix diced chicken, potatoes, carrots, peas, onions, and cream sauce. Heat and serve on toast or hot biscuits.
Serves 7 to 8

(Opposite page) James Maier, right, executive chef of Edison Institute in Dearborn, invited me to his office in the Education Building to talk about Henry Ford and his soybean research. Chef Maier wanted to hear about my experiences working for Mr. Ford, and what his favorite foods were. He planned to incorporate recipes of that time into the menus of Edison Institute restaurants, including the new village restaurant, Taste of History, to give visitors a history as well as culinary experience. This picture was taken before a painting of Mr. and Mrs. Henry Ford in Lovett Hall, 1993. Photograph courtesy of Edison Institute

Fried Chicken

3/4 c. vegetable shortening or oil
1 egg
2 Tbs. milk
!/2 tsp. salt
1/8 tsp. pepper
1/8 tsp. paprika
12 pieces chicken (legs and thighs)
1/2 c. flour

Heat frying pan and oil to 225 to 250 degrees. Combine egg, milk, salt, pepper, and paprika. Coat chicken parts with egg mixture. Dip chicken into flour. Shake off excess. Fry for 8 to 9 minutes. Turn chicken and continue until desired brownness is obtained.
Yields 4 servings

Turkey à la King

1/2 lb. butter (or margarine)
1 c. flour
4 c. hot water
4 c. warm milk
1 Tbs. turkey base
1 1/2 lb. diced cooked turkey
5 oz. diced red pepper
1 green pepper, diced and blanched
8 oz. mushrooms (pieces and stems)
1/3 tsp. salt
1/4 tsp. pepper

Melt butter in saucepan at low heat. Add flour and stir constantly with a wire whip for 2 minutes to make a roux. Add hot water, milk, and turkey base to roux, stirring constantly (to make nice and smooth) for about 3 minutes. Add diced turkey, red pepper, green pepper, mushrooms, salt, and pepper. Fold the ingredients together gently. Serve on rice, hot biscuits, or on patty shells.
Serves 7 to 8

Chicken or Turkey Gravy

4 c. milk
1/3 c. flour
1 level tsp. salt
1/3 tsp. pepper
1/3 c. melted butter (or margarine)

Place half the milk in a screw-top jar, add the flour, salt, and pepper. Shake until the mix is well blended. Melt butter (or margarine) and remaining two cups of milk in a saucepan. Combine all ingredients and cook slowly for 4 to 5 minutes, until well thickened. Keep gravy warm.
Yields 4 cups of gravy

Bread Stuffing for Poultry, Pork, or Fish

1 lb. stale soy (or white) bread
2 c. cold water
3/4 c. diced onion
1/2 c. diced celery
3/4 c. soy bean oil (or margarine)
2 tsp. salt
2 tsp. sage
2 tsp. poultry seasoning
2 Tbs. chopped parsley

Preheat oven to 350 degrees.
Cut bread into 1-inch cubes, soak in cold water for 5 minutes and drain. Sauté onion and celery in oil until tender. Combine vegetables, bread cubes, and seasonings. Place in pan, cover with greased wax paper. Bake 30–45 minutes.
Serves 10

Perch Fillets

6 perch fillets
1/3 tsp. salt
1/3 tsp. pepper
1 Tbs. lemon juice
1/3 c. oil (or melted margarine)

Sprinkle fish with salt, pepper, and lemon juice. Heat oil to 350 degrees and fry fish for about 3 minutes. Turn fish and fry another 3 minutes. Drain fish on paper towels and serve while still warm.

Baby perch merchandising names: fillet, shell pink perch, coral perch, or fillet of fish.
Yields 6 servings

Cod Fillets, Plain or Breaded

4 6-oz. cod fillets
1/2 tsp. salt
1/2 tsp. black pepper
1/2 c. vegetable oil
1 Tbs. chopped parsley
1 fresh lemon

If served plain: Season fish with salt and pepper. Fry fish in oil for 3 minutes on each side until golden brown. Serve with a little parsley and sliced lemon.

If served breaded: Dip each fish piece in 3/4 cup flour mixed with salt and pepper. Bake at 375 degrees in a greased pan for 6 to 7 minutes on one side. Turn the fish and bake for 3 to 5 minutes longer, until golden brown.
Yields 4 servings

Old-Fashioned Codfish Cakes

1 lb. salted codfish
5 medium-sized unpeeled potatoes
2 eggs
1/2 c. vegetable shortening
2 Tbs. minced onions
1 tsp. nutmeg (or mace)
1 tsp. grated rind of lemon

Soak the codfish in cold water for 4 hours or overnight. Cut into strips. Place strips in a saucepan and cover with fresh water. Bring water to a boil, pour off the water and repeat with fresh cold water. When water comes to a boil, reduce heat and simmer for 15 minutes. Drain, squeeze out the moisture, and set aside. Boil the potatoes 20 to 25 minutes until well done. Remove the skin and rice potatoes into a bowl. Mix in codfish, eggs, vegetable shortening, minced onion, nutmeg (or mace), and grated lemon rind. Shape into small or medium-sized cakes, or scoop mixture with tablespoon and drop into hot oil. Fry until golden brown. For a nice change the fish cakes can be dipped into flour, both sides, or rolled into fine bread crumbs before frying in hot oil 2 to 3 minutes on each side.
Yields 5 servings

Baked Breaded Fish Fillets

1 lb. or 4 4-oz. fillets of haddock or perch
1/2 c. cream (or evaporated milk)
1 tsp. salt
1/8 tsp. black pepper
3/4 c. fine ground bread crumbs

Preheat oven to 375 degrees.
Dip each piece of fish in mixture of cream (or evaporated milk), salt, and pepper. Roll each piece of fish in the fine bread crumbs. Place fish in greased baking pan and bake for 15 to 20 minutes until golden brown. Serve with some tartar sauce.
Yields 4 servings

Seafood Quiche

7 whole eggs
3 c. milk (or light cream)
1 Tbs. cornstarch
1/2 tsp. salt
1/2 tsp. mace
1 Tbs. white wine
2 c. diced crabmeat (cooked)
2 c. diced shrimp (cooked)
1 1/2 c. diced asparagus tips
2 8-inch pastry shells

Preheat oven to 350 degrees.
Blend together eggs, milk (or cream), cornstarch, salt, mace, and wine. Add crabmeat, shrimp, and diced asparagus tips. Mix. Pour mixed filling into partly baked pastry shells. Bake 35 to 40 minutes until golden brown.
Yields 2 8-inch quiches

Quiche Lorraine

6 or 7 whole eggs
3 c. milk (or coffee cream)
1/2 tsp. salt
1/2 tsp. nutmeg
1 Tbs. cornstarch
3 c. shredded Swiss cheese
1 c. shredded Monterey Jack cheese
1 1/2 c. mushroom stems and pieces
1 1/2 c. crumbled cooked bacon

Preheat oven to 350 degrees.
Blend together eggs, milk (or cream), salt, nutmeg, and cornstarch for 2 minutes. Add shredded cheeses, mushrooms, and crumbled bacon. Pour mix into 3 partly baked 8-inch pie shells and bake 35 to 40 minutes until golden brown.
Yields three 8-inch quiches

Vegetable Quiche

6 whole eggs
1 c. milk
1 tsp. salt
1 c. chopped spinach
1 tsp. cornstarch
1/2 tsp. nutmeg
1 1/2 c. shredded Swiss cheese
1 1/2 c. shredded Monterey Jack cheese

Preheat oven to 350 degrees.
Blend together eggs, milk, and salt. Beat for 2 minutes. Add chopped spinach, cornstarch, nutmeg, and shredded cheeses. Pour mixed filling into partly baked pastry shell. Bake for 35 to 40 minutes until golden brown.
Yields 1 10-inch quiche

Poor Man's Lobster Patties

4 tsp. finely chopped onions
Soybean oil or butter
1 1/2 lb. freshly boiled, riced, and whipped potatoes
1 tsp. salt
1/2 tsp. pepper
3 Tbs. lobster base (found in gourmet food stores) dissolved in
1/3 c. water
2 or 3 whole eggs well beaten
2 level Tbs. cornstarch

Sauté onion in a little soybean oil or butter (do not brown). Add to the whipped potatoes, along with salt, pepper, and the dissolved lobster base. Add the eggs. Mix by hand or machine and chill in the refrigerator. Form the mixture into patties or little balls. Deep fry or pan fry at 375 degrees until golden brown.
Yields 9 4-ounce patties

Shrimp Creole or Shrimp Sauce

1/2 c. butter (or soy margarine)
1/2 c. sliced onions (1 inch long and 1/5 inch thick)
1/3 c. sliced green peppers (1 inch long)
1/3 c. diced celery (cut 1/8 inch thick and 1 inch long)
1/3 c. mushrooms
1 lb. shrimp (cooked, peeled, and deveined)
2 c. hot water
1 tsp. shrimp (or fish) base (found in gourmet food stores)

In a heavy saucepan, melt butter (or soy margarine). Add onions, peppers, and diced celery. Sauté and stir for 3 minutes. Add mushrooms and remaining ingredients. Simmer for 5 minutes. Serve hot over cooked rice.
Yields 4 to 5 servings

Baked or Broiled Salmon Steak

4 6-oz salmon steaks
1/2 tsp. salt
1/2 tsp. black pepper
1/4 c. melted butter
1 sliced lemon
1 tsp. chopped parsley

Preheat oven to 400 degrees.
Season salmon with salt and pepper. Brush with melted butter. Bake for 15 to 18 minutes until almost done. Remove the bone and skin carefully. Decorate with sliced lemon and chopped parsley and a little pan gravy.
Yields 4 servings

Salmon Dish

1 (8-oz.) can salmon
1/2 c. rich (or canned) milk
1 c. shredded cheese
2 eggs
1 Tbs. chopped parsley
1 Tbs. lemon juice
1 tsp. salt
1/4 tsp. pepper
1/2 c. diced fine onions

Preheat oven to 375 degrees.
Remove bone and skin from the salmon and mix with remaining ingredients. Bake in greased 2-quart dish for 15 to 20 minutes.
Yields 4 to 5 servings

Salmon Loaf

1 (15-oz.) can salmon
1/2 c. mayonnaise
1 (10 oz.) can cream of celery soup
1/2 c. finely chopped onion
1/2 c. chopped green pepper
1 Tbs. lemon juice
1 tsp. salt
1 egg well beaten
1 c. fine dry bread crumbs
melted butter
lemon slices

Preheat oven to 350 degrees.
Flake drained salmon and mix with mayonnaise, cream of celery soup, chopped onion, green pepper, lemon juice, salt, egg, and bread crumbs. Pour into a greased 9- by 5-inch loaf pan. Bake for 20 to 25 minutes and serve with a little melted butter. Top with a slice of lemon.
Yields 7 to 8 servings

City Chicken

1 lb. fresh ground pork
1 lb. fresh ground veal
1/2 c. beef stock or water
1/2 c. dry bread crumbs
2 eggs (beaten)
1 level tsp. salt
1 level tsp. pepper
pinch ground sage
4 skewers (round sticks)
1 egg with a pinch of salt beaten in 1/3 cup of milk
1 c. fine bread crumbs

Preheat oven to 300 degrees.
Combine pork, veal, stock, 1/2 cup dry bread crumbs, 2 beaten eggs, salt, pepper, and sage. Mix in mixer at low speed for 1 minute with a flat paddle. Shape into drumsticks on skewers. Mix remaining beaten egg, salt, and milk. Dip meat in mixture and roll in fine bread crumbs. Bake in deep pan with small amount of water for 30 to 45 minutes.
Yields 4 portions

Mock Chicken Legs

2 lb. pork (cubed)
6 oz. veal (cubed)
6 wooden skewers
2 eggs
1/2 c. milk
1 c. fine bread crumbs
1 tsp. salt
1/3 tsp. pepper

Preheat oven to 325 degrees.
Place cubes of meat (three pork and two veal) on 6 skewers, alternating meats. Beat eggs and milk. Season bread crumbs with salt and pepper. Dip mock chicken legs into egg and milk mixture and roll in bread crumbs. Place in baking pans, add 1/4 inch water, and cover. Bake for 30 to 45 minutes, or until meat is tender and well done. Leave cover off during the last 15 minutes if the meat has not browned.
Yields 6 servings

Hawaiian Style Veal Steaks

6 4- to 5-oz. veal steaks
seasoned flour
vegetable oil
1 c. pineapple tidbits
1/3 tsp. ground ginger
1/2 c. diced fine green pepper
1 tomato (cut up fine)

Preheat oven to 350 degrees.
Dredge veal steak in flour seasoned with salt and pepper. Brown in skillet in small amount of vegetable oil or deep fry. Place steak in baking pan. Combine remaining ingredients and pour over veal steak. Bake for 30 to 35 minutes or until tender.
Yields 6 servings

Boston Style Veal Cutlets

1 c. flour
2 tsp. salt
1/2 tsp. pepper
10 (6 oz.) veal cutlets
vegetable oil

Sauce
1/2 c. soybean oil
dash garlic powder
2 Tbs. flour
3 c. milk
2 Tbs. Worcestershire sauce
1 tsp. salt

Preheat oven to 350 degrees.
Combine flour, salt, and pepper. Dredge cutlets in flour mixture and brown in small amount of oil in skillet. Place cutlets in baking pans. Cover and bake 15 minutes.

Sauce
Heat oil. Add garlic and blend in flour. Add milk, stir, and cook. Blend in Worcestershire sauce and salt. Remove veal from oven and cover with sauce. Return to 300-degree oven, uncovered, for 15 to 20 minutes.
Yields 10 6-ounce servings

Baked Ham with Dressing

1/4 c. chopped onions
1/4 c. chopped green peppers
3/4 c. vegetable shortening
1 c. diced celery
4 c. bread cubes (or crumbs)
1/3 tsp. pepper
10 slices ham
1/4 c. mustard

Preheat oven to 350 degrees.
Cook chopped onion and peppers in shortening. Add celery, bread cubes, and pepper. Place five slices of ham on a baking pan and spread with mustard. Divide dressing over the 5 ham slices. Place another slice of ham directly over the dressing. Pour some mushroom sauce over everything. (See Brown Mushroom Sauce.) Bake 35 to 40 minutes.
Yields 5 portions

Ham and Apple Casserole

1/2 level tsp. ground cloves
1 c. brown sugar
2 c. sliced apples
1 1/4 lb. diced cooked ham
1 Tbs. cornstarch
1/4 c. lemon juice
3/4 c. water
1 c. bread or cake crumbs

Preheat oven to 350 degrees.
Mix cloves and brown sugar. Arrange alternate layers of apples, sugar mixture, and ham in a baking dish or pan. Mix cornstarch, lemon juice, and water and pour over apples and diced ham. Cover with bread or cake crumbs. Bake for 45 minutes. Cover baking dish the last 15 minutes.
Yields 5 portions

Old-Fashioned Baked Pork Chops

8 (4 oz.) pork chops
1 c. flour
1 tsp. salt
1/2 tsp. pepper
vegetable shortening to grease pan
2 c. water
1 tsp. chicken base

Preheat oven to 400 degrees.
Mix flour, salt, and pepper. Dredge pork chops through seasoned flour. Place pork chops on a well-greased pan and brown and bake them 15 minutes or until well done. Or, do it Grandma's way: Place pork chops, browned on both sides, in a baking dish. Cover them with 4 cups chicken stock and bake at 375 degrees for about 1 hour.
Yields 8 chops

Savory Pork Chops

6 4-oz. pork chops
vegetable oil
2 tsp. salt
1/3 tsp. pepper
1/2 tsp. paprika
1 c. orange juice
1 tbs. brown sugar
1 tsp. cinnamon
1 orange (sliced)
1/2 tsp. whole cloves

Preheat oven to 350 degrees.
Brown pork chops in small amount of oil. Sprinkle chops with mixture of salt, pepper, and paprika. Arrange in baking pan. Combine orange juice, brown sugar, and cinnamon. Pour over chops, cover, and bake for 1 hour. Garnish with orange slices and cloves.
Yields 6 4-ounce servings

Pork Chops with Rice

12 4-oz. pork chops
1/2 c. flour
vegetable oil
3/4 c. uncooked rice
1/4 c. chopped celery
1/4 c. green pepper
1/4 c. chopped onion
1 can tomatoes (or two whole tomatoes)
1 tsp. Worcestershire sauce
1 tsp. salt
1 tsp. sugar
1 1/2 c. fine bread crumbs

Preheat oven to 325 degrees.
Dredge chops in flour. Brown in a little vegetable oil. Cook rice according to package directions for 10 minutes. Drain. Sauté celery, green pepper, and onions in vegetable oil. Add tomatoes, rice, and seasonings. Mix well and place in greased pan. Place pork chops on top and sprinkle with bread crumbs. Bake for 30 to 40 minutes.
Yields 12 portions

Breaded Baked Pork Chops

12 3-oz. pork chops
1 c. flour
1 tsp. salt
1/3 tsp. pepper
2 eggs beaten
3 c. fine bread crumbs
Vegetable shortening to grease pan

Preheat oven to 350 degrees.
Mix flour, salt, and pepper. Dredge pork chops in mixture. Dip floured chops into beaten eggs, and then into bread crumbs. Place pork chops in well-greased baking pan. Bake for 30 minutes. Cover the chops if they become dry or too brown. (Or fry chops on top of the range in vegetable oil.)
Yields 12 servings

Pork Chops Hawaiian with Rice Patties

Pork Chops
12 3-oz. pork chops
3/4 c. flour
1 tsp. salt
1/4 tsp. pepper
vegetable oil
1/2 c. water
1/4 c. cider vinegar
1/4 c. brown sugar
1/2 tsp. salt
1 Tbs. soy sauce
1/2 c. pineapple juice
1 Tbs. cornstarch

Rice Patties
1 c. rice
2 c. water
1 tsp. salt
1 Tbs. margarine
2 eggs (slightly beaten)
1 tsp. salt
1/2 tsp. pepper

Preheat oven to 350 degrees.

Pork Chops
Dredge pork chops in flour, salt, and pepper mixture and brown in a little hot oil. Place chops in baking pan. Combine and heat water, vinegar, brown sugar, salt, soy sauce, and pineapple juice. Mix cornstarch in a little water and add to hot liquid. Cook until slightly thick. Pour sauce over chops, cover, and bake for 30 minutes. Serve with rice patties.

Rice Patties
Place rice in a 12-inch square pan with water. Add 1 teaspoon salt and margarine. Cover and bake or steam for 20 minutes. Beat eggs, add salt and pepper and mix with cooked rice. Shape into 6 patties or balls. Bake in a shallow pan for 20 minutes, covered.
Yields 6 servings

Braised Liver with Onions

1/3 c. flour
3 tsp. salt
1/2 tsp. pepper
1 1/2 lb. thin sliced beef liver
1 1/2 c. sliced onions
1/2 c. vegetable oil (or bacon fat)
1 c. water

Preheat oven to 350 degrees.
Mix flour, salt, and pepper. Dredge liver in the flour mixture and brown in hot oil or bacon fat. Sauté sliced onions in oil until translucent. Place liver in a baking pan. Cover with sautéed onions and add the water. Cover and bake for 15 to 25 minutes.
Yields 8 to 10 portions

Tomato, Egg, and Rice Casserole

1 c. uncooked white rice
4 sliced hard-boiled eggs
1 c. grated Cheddar cheese
1/2 tsp. paprika
1 Tbs. salt
1/4 c. chopped green pepper
1/4 c. fine chopped onion
vegetable oil
3 c. tomato sauce (or tomato purée)

Preheat oven to 325 degrees.
Cook rice according to package directions. Add sliced, hard-boiled eggs, grated cheese, paprika, and salt to the rice. Brown green pepper and onion lightly in oil and add to mixture. Add tomato sauce and mix well. Place in 2-quart baking dish and bake 30 to 35 minutes (or bake in individual casseroles). Serve with mushroom or celery sauce. (See Basic Medium White Sauce variations.)
Yields 8 servings

Cheese Soufflé

1/2 c. butter
1/2 c. flour
2 c. hot milk
1 tsp. salt
2 c. grated Cheddar cheese
5 egg yolks (slightly beaten)
5 egg whites
1/2 tsp. cream of tartar

Preheat oven to 350 degrees.
Melt butter, add flour, and blend. Add two cups hot milk and stir until smooth. Add salt. Add cheese and stir until melted. Add slightly beaten egg yolks, alternating hot mixture and egg mixture. Cool. Beat the egg whites and cream of tartar until stiff but not dry. Fold into cooled mixture. Place in individual casseroles or cups greased on the bottom only. Bake until set, about 15 minutes.
Yields 5 to 6 servings

Vegetable Cheese Casserole

4 c. diced potatoes
2 c. diced carrots
1/2 c. diced small onions
1 c. diced small celery
1/2 c. butter (or margarine)
1/2 c. flour
3 c. milk
3 c. grated Cheddar cheese
1 tsp. salt
1/2 tsp. pepper
1 box frozen peas
1 c. cracker crumbs

Preheat oven to 350 degrees.
Boil diced potatoes, carrots, onions, and celery for 15 to 20 minutes. Make a creamsauce with butter, flour, and milk. Add the cheese, stirring until cheese is melted. Season with salt and pepper. Mix peas, cooked vegetables, and sauce. Place mixture in baking dish or individual casseroles and top with cracker crumbs. Bake 20 to 25 minutes.
Yields 8 to 10 servings

Cheesy Egg Noodle Loaf

12 oz. egg noodles
5 c. water
3 Tbs. salt
1 c. cracker (or bread) crumbs
1/2 lb. grated Cheddar cheese
6 slightly beaten eggs
1/3 c. finely chopped onions

1/2 tsp. salt
1/4 tsp. pepper
1/4 tsp. paprika
1/3 c. butter
2 c. milk
1/4 c. chopped green pepper
1/4 c. chopped pimiento

Preheat oven to 350 degrees.
Cook noodles in 5 cups salted (3 tablespoons) water for 4 minutes. Rinse in cold water and drain. Combine noodles with all other ingredients and mix thoroughly. Place mixture in 2-quart baking dish, and bake 45 minutes. Serve with 2-ounce portion of mushroom, celery, or almond sauce. (See Basic Medium White Sauce variations.)
Yields 10 servings

Spaghetti Meat Casserole

1 lb. spaghetti
2 quarts salted water
1/2 c. chopped onions
1/3 c. chopped green peppers
1/3 c. chopped pimientos
1/2 c. butter (or margarine), divided
1 1/4 lb. ground beef

1 tsp. salt
1/2 tsp. pepper
1/2 tsp. paprika
1 Tbs. Worcestershire sauce
1 c. tomato purée
1 c. water
1 c. grated cheese

Preheat oven to 350 degrees.
Cook spaghetti 20 minutes in two quarts of salted water. Drain. Cook onion, green peppers, and pimientos slowly in butter until tender. Sauté or cook ground beef in margarine, also. Add vegetables, salt, pepper, paprika, Worcestershire sauce, tomato purée, and water to meat. Combine spaghetti with meat mix. Add the cheese. Place mix in 2-quart buttered dish and bake 40 minutes.
Yields 6 servings

Spaghetti Tomato Casserole

1 1/2 lb. spaghetti
3 qt. boiling water
1 Tbs. salt
2 Tbs. chopped onion
1 Tbs. vegetable oil
2 Tbs. flour
small tomato, peeled and diced

2 c. sliced mushrooms (can or fresh)
1 tsp. salt
1/3 tsp. pepper
1/2 tsp. oregano
1 c. bread crumbs
1 c. grated cheese

Preheat oven to 325 degrees.
Cook spaghetti for 3 minutes in boiling, salted (1 tablespoon) water. Sauté onions in oil. Add flour and blend. Add tomato, mushrooms, and seasonings. Cook 8 minutes. Mix with spaghetti. Put in 2-quart baking dish or individual casseroles. Sprinkle mixture of crumbs and cheese on top. Bake 30 to 40 minutes.
Yields 1 2-quart casserole

Chow Mein

1 lb. cubed pork
1 lb. cubed veal
1/4 c. flour
1/3 c. shortening divided
3 tsp. salt
1/2 tsp. pepper
1/3 c. chopped onions
1 1/2 c. diced celery

1 c. diced tomatoes
little soy sauce to taste
1 c. meat stock (or chicken broth)
1 Tbs. flour
1/2 c. water
Worcestershire, optional
1 (#2 1/2 can) chop suey vegetables
Chinese noodles or cooked rice

Dredge meat in flour and brown in part of melted shortening. Season with salt and pepper. Sauté onions and celery in melted shortening and add to meat. Combine meat, onions, celery, tomatoes, soy sauce, and meat stock and simmer 1 hour. Make paste of flour and cold water and add to chow mein mix. Add Worcestershire sauce if desired. Cook 45 minutes longer. Add chop suey vegetables and heat mixture. Serve over Chinese noodles or cooked rice.
Yields 8 servings

Food chemists Austin Curtis, left, assistant to Dr. Carver, and Robert Smith, right, sample soybean food I served at a soybean brunch at the Henry Ford Estate–Fair Lane in 1988. Photograph courtesy of Jan Willemse

Egg Foo Yung

1/2 lb. cooked meat (or cooked shrimp) cut in strips
1/2 lb. celery cut in long, narrow 1 1/3-inch strips
1/2 lb. onions sliced thin lengthwise
Vegetable oil
1/2 lb. bean sprouts drained
10 eggs (well beaten)
1 tsp. salt
1/3 tsp. pepper

Sauté celery and onions in small amount of oil. Add meat and bean sprouts and heat mixture. Beat eggs and add salt and pepper. Heat an 8-inch skillet until very hot and add a small amount of oil. Add enough egg mixture to cover bottom of skillet. Cook until egg is solid and place a scoop of meat mixture on half the cooked egg. Fold egg over meat mixture. Brown on both sides and place in baking pan to keep warm until serving time. Serve with rice and two ounces of beef gravy.
Yields 8 to 10 portions

S A U C E S

Basic Medium White Sauce

1/2 c. butter (or margarine)
1/3 c. all purpose flour
1 level tsp. white pepper
4 c. hot milk

Melt butter (or margarine) in heavy skillet. Blend in flour and pepper. Cook slowly for 2 minutes, stirring constantly over low heat, to make the roux. Add 4 cups of hot milk, stirring briskly until it becomes nice and smooth. Simmer for 3 minutes. Strain through a fine sieve if you want a very smooth sauce. This sauce could be used for egg sauce by adding chopped eggs, or shrimp sauce by adding chopped shrimp, and many other sauces by adding different flavoring agents such as sautéed mushrooms, celery, or sliced almonds.
Yields 4 cups

Mother's Basic White Sauce

3 c. milk, divided
2 Tbs. butter (or oleo)
1 tsp. salt
1/2 tsp. pepper
1/3 c. flour (or 1 heaping teaspoon cornstarch)

Heat 2 cups milk, butter, salt, and pepper. Bring to boiling point. Dissolve 1/3 cup flour (or one heaping teaspoon cornstarch) in remaining 1 cup of milk. Mix well and add to the boiling milk and cook slowly for 2 minutes, stirring constantly until smooth.
Yields 3 1/2 cups rich white sauce

Brown Mushroom Sauce

3 oz. melted butter (or margarine)
1 small onion finely chopped
1/2 lb. sliced mushroom
1/3 c. flour
4 c. beef stock
1/4 c. sherry wine
1/4 tsp. salt

Melt butter (or margarine) and sauté onions and mushrooms slowly until tender. Dissolve the flour in beef stock and mix with sherry wine and salt. Slowly add this to the sautéed onions and mushrooms. Bring to a boil.
Yields 4 1/2 cups

Raisin Sauce for Ham

1 c. butter
2/3 c. sherry wine
1 Tbs. real lemon juice
1/4 tsp. salt
1/2 tsp. ground cloves
1 Tbs. flour
2 c. applesauce
1 c. raisins
1/2 c. currant jelly

Melt butter in saucepan. Mix the wine, lemon juice, salt, cloves, and flour. Mix well. Add the rest of ingredients and bring to a boil. If the sauce is too heavy, add a little more sherry wine. Very good with ham dinners.
Yields 3 1/2 cups

Holiday Ham Glaze

1 c. brown sugar
1/2 c. prepared mustard

Mix sugar and mustard. Brush on ham before placing in oven. The glaze makes a nice outer crust and adds a very good flavor to the ham.

Brandy Sauce

2 c. water
1/2 c. brown sugar
1/2 c. confectioners' sugar
1/4 tsp. salt
1 orange—rind and juice
1 lemon—rind and juice
2 Tbs. cornstarch
1 c. water
1/2 c. brandy

Bring to a boil the water, brown sugar, confectioners' sugar, salt, orange and lemon rind and juice. Simmer for a few minutes. Dissolve cornstarch in water and add slowly to boiling mixture until slightly thickened. Remove from heat, stir in brandy, and serve over cakes or puddings.
Yields 4 cups

Sweet Duck Sauce

1 (10-oz.) can apricots
1 (10-oz.) can purple plums
1 Tbs. molasses
3 Tbs. honey
1/4 tsp. ground ginger
1/4 tsp. salt

Drain fruit and reserve liquid. Purée fruit. Add all remaining ingredients, including reserved fruit juices, and bring almost to a boil.
Yields 2 cups

Shrimp Sauce

Fish of your choice
1 1/2 c. hot water
1 Tbs. shrimp base (found in gourmet food stores)
2 Tbs. butter
2 Tbs. flour
1/8 tsp. paprika
1/2 c. hot, heavy cream (or hot half-and-half)
1 Tbs. sauterne wine

Combine hot water and shrimp base and mix well to make poaching broth. Poach fish of your choice using enough broth to barely cover the fish. Melt butter over low heat. Blend in flour and add remaining poaching broth, paprika, cream, and wine. Mix well.
Yields 2 cups

Seafood Dip or Seafood Sauce

1 lemon—grated rind and juice
2 Tbs. horseradish
1 c. tomato paste
1 c. barbecue sauce
1/8 tsp. salt

Blend together all ingredients. Mix well and chill. Good for seafood or dips.
Yields 2 cups

Clam Cream Sauce

1/4 c. butter
1/2 c. flour
4 c. clam juice
1 Tbs. clam base (can be found in gourmet food stores)
1 c. chopped clams
2 Tbs. sherry wine
1/2 c. cream (half-and-half)

Melt butter over slow heat. Do not brown. Blend in flour. Add clam juice and clam base. Cook for a few minutes, stirring constantly. Add the chopped clams, sherry wine, and cream. Keep hot in a double boiler or hot water bath. Good with fish dishes.
Yields 6 cups

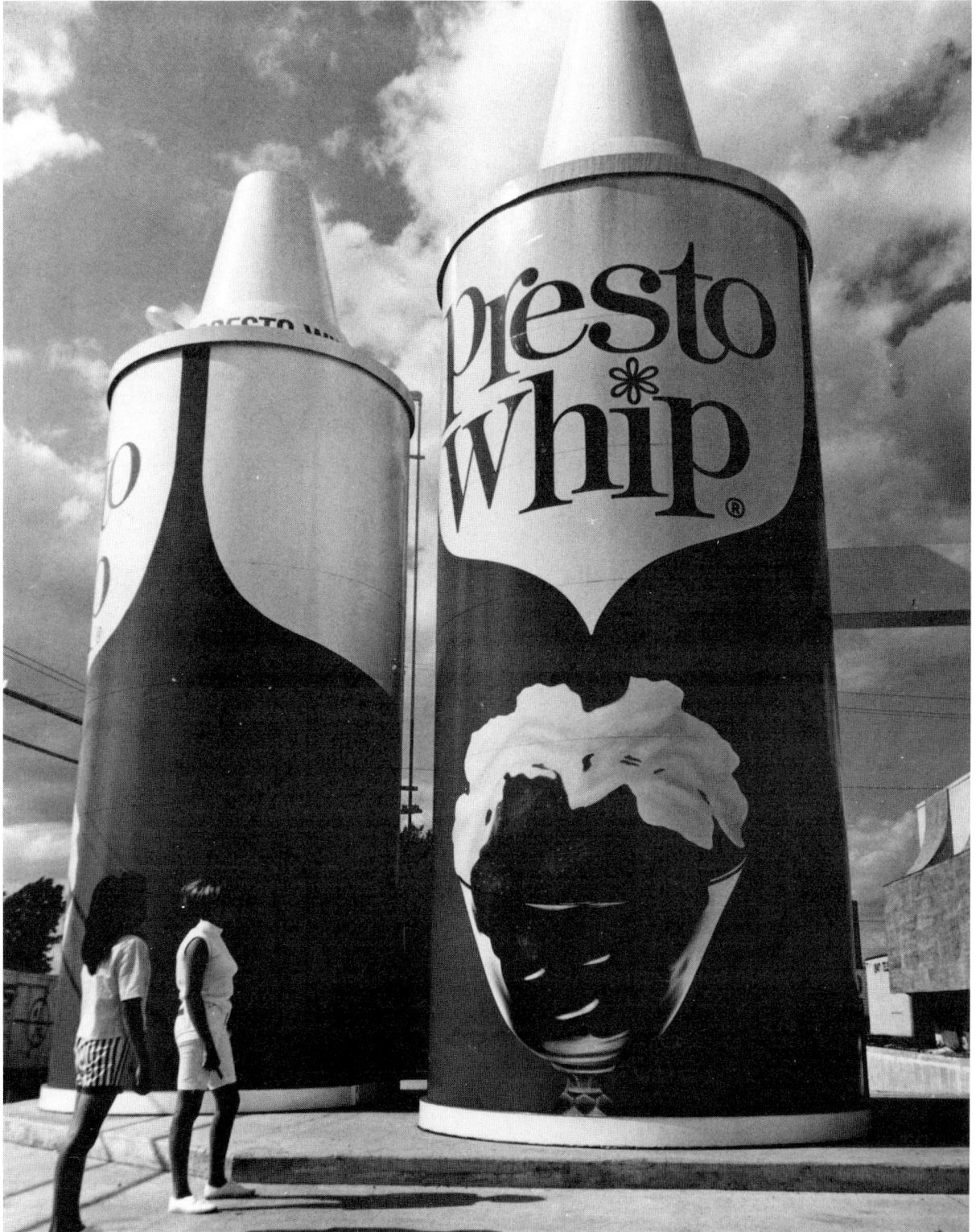

Spicy All-Purpose Sauce

1/2 c. butter
1/2 c. fine diced onion
1/2 c. fine diced celery
1 c. tomato purée
1 c. barbecue sauce
1/2 tsp. salt
1/3 tsp. pepper
1 Tbs. brown sugar

In a heavy kettle, melt butter, sauté onions and celery until tender. Be careful not to burn. Combine all ingredients, bring to a boil, and simmer for 15 to 20 minutes. Can be served with beef, fowl, or fish.
Yields 3 cups

Lyonnaise Sauce

1 1/2 c. butter (or margarine)
1 large sliced onion
4 c. water
1 Tbs. espagnole base (can be found in gourmet food stores, or substitute beef base)
1/4 tsp. salt
1/8 tsp. pepper

Melt butter (or margarine) and sauté onions until golden brown. Add water and soup base. Boil for 2 or 3 minutes. Add salt and pepper. Serve with beef, short ribs, or liver.
Yields 4 cups

(Opposite page) These giant Presto Whip cans attracted the attention of motorists on Telegraph Road, south of Michigan Avenue, for many years, but not many people knew of their connection to Henry Ford. Stored inside the structures were soybean oil and sugar used to make the substitute cream for the whip. The product was the result of experiments with soybeans by Robert Smith, food chemist, at the request of Mr. Ford. Photograph courtesy of the Dearborn Historical Commission.

Barbecue Sauce

1 #10 can tomato sauce (13 cups)
1/4 c. cider
1/2 c. diced onion
1 tsp. liquid smoked seasoning
1 Tbs. prepared mustard
1/2 c. soy sauce
3 Tbs. Worcestershire sauce

Blend all ingredients in a heavy saucepan. Bring to a boil and simmer slowly for about 5 to 10 minutes. Good to serve with chicken, spareribs, or pork chops.
Yields 4 quarts

Peter Veach, executive chef at the Henry Ford Estate, and I show soybean cookies we baked for an all-soybean luncheon for the press held at Fair Lane in 1990. Photograph by Eleanor Eaton

Vegetables

Baby Small Carrots

4 c. water
2 Tbs. sugar
1/2 tsp. salt
3 lb. baby carrots, fresh or frozen
4 Tbs. butter
pepper

Bring water, sugar, and salt to a boil, then add the baby carrots. Bring back to the boiling point and cook the carrots for 5 to 7 minutes. Drain the water from the carrots. Add 4 tablespoons of butter and a little pepper. Put carrots in the oven to keep warm. Serve hot. The addition of cooked peas makes a nice combination.
Yields 7 to 9 servings

Fresh Orange Carrots

1 lb. fresh carrots
1/4 c. butter (or margarine)
1/2 tsp. salt
1/3 tsp. nutmeg
1 tsp. honey (or sugar)
1/3 c. orange juice (or water)

Slice or grate cleaned carrots and boil them until partially done. Drain. Melt butter (or margarine) in medium-sized heavy pan. Add salt, nutmeg, honey (or sugar), and orange juice (or water). Mix and add carrots. Cook over medium heat until carrots are somewhat crispy, but tender. Garnish with thin slice of orange and parsley sprigs.
Yields 3 or 4 servings

Fresh Carrots

1 lb. medium-sized carrots
3 c. water
1 Tbs. butter (or soybean margarine)
1/8 tsp. salt
1/8 tsp. black pepper
1 Tbs. clean chopped parsley

Clean carrots, and cut into 2-inch sticks (or slice them). Place carrots in three cups of water. Boil them for about 10 minutes until barely done and drain. Add to the carrots 1 tablespoon butter (or soybean margarine), salt, pepper, and toss a little. Sprinkle with some clean chopped parsley.
Yields 4 portions

Glazed Carrots

15 medium to small carrots
6 c. salted water
3 Tbs. margarine (or butter)
3 Tbs. honey
1 Tbs. brown sugar
1/2 tsp. salt

Preheat oven to 375 degrees.
Cook whole carrots 10 minutes in 1 1/2-quart pan with 6 cups of salted water and drain. Place almost-cooked carrots in a baking pan. While carrots are cooking, melt margarine (or butter) in a saucepan. Add honey, brown sugar, and salt. Pour mixture over drained carrots. Bake carrots about 10 minutes. Turn carrots. Bake 5 or 6 minutes more.
Yields 4 or 5 portions

Cauliflower

2 lbs. cauliflower, frozen or fresh
boiling salted water
2 heaping Tbs. butter melted
1/8 tsp. salt
1/8 tsp. pepper

Place cauliflower in rapidly boiling water. When water returns to boil, reduce heat and cook until just tender. Do not overcook. Drain well. Add butter and seasoning.
Yields 6 to 8 servings

Brussels Sprouts

2 lbs. Brussels sprouts
2 Tbs. butter (or soybean margarine)
1/8 tsp. salt
1/8 tsp. pepper

Remove discolored outer leaves of Brussels sprouts, trim stem ends, and wash thoroughly. Soak in cold, salted water. Drain well and place in boiling salted water. When water returns to a boil, simmer for 10 minutes or until tender. Drain off water. Add butter, and season with salt and pepper before serving.
Yields 6 servings

Savory Oven-Browned Potatoes

4 lbs. potatoes—skin on
1/2 c. butter (or vegetable oil)
1/3 c. Worcestershire sauce
3 tsp. salt
1 Tbs. paprika

Preheat oven to 400 degrees.
Scrub potatoes with a brush in cold water and cut into uniform pieces. Boil potatoes 15 minutes. Place in shallow baking pan. Mix melted butter and Worcestershire sauce and pour over potatoes. Mix salt and paprika and sprinkle over potatoes. Bake for 20 to 25 minutes or until potatoes are done and nicely browned.
Yields 10 servings

Cabbage

2 lbs. cabbage
boiling salted water
1/2 c. butter (or margarine)
some celery seeds

Wash and trim cabbage. Remove core and cut into 3-ounce wedges (or shred coarsely). Cook cabbage 5 minutes in boiling, salted water. Remove from heat and cover for about 7 minutes. Drain cabbage well and sauté lightly in butter. Toss with celery seeds and serve. Cabbage should be tender, but retain some texture and shape.
Yields 6 to 8 servings

Candied Sweet Potatoes

5 lb. unpeeled sweet potatoes
1 c. maple syrup
1/2 c. butter
2 tsp. salt
1 c. cider
1/2 c. water

Preheat oven to 350 degrees.
Boil or steam sweet potatoes 20 minutes. Cool and peel, then slice 3/4-inch thick. Arrange sliced potatoes in baking pan. Mix other ingredients and boil 5 minutes. Pour mixture over sweet potatoes and bake 25 to 30 minutes.
Yields 10 portions

Fresh Sweet Potatoes or Yams

1 1/2 lb. peeled sweet potatoes
3/4 c. brown sugar
1/2 c. melted margarine
1/3 tsp. salt
1/8 tsp. black pepper
1/2 c. cream (or canned milk)
1/4 c. flour

Preheat oven to 350 degrees.
Cook sweet potatoes in salted water 20 minutes or until done. Mash or whip sweet potatoes, and add brown sugar, margarine, salt, pepper, and mix a little. Add cream (or canned milk) and flour. Place mixture in buttered casserole dish and bake for about 30 to 35 minutes.
Yields 4 portions

Picnic Baked Potatoes

2 large baking potatoes
2 Tbs. melted butter
1/2 c. freshly grated cheese
1/8 tsp. salt
1/8 tsp. pepper
paprika

Preheat oven to 350 degrees.
Clean potatoes, leaving skin on (do not peel). Cut crosswise into 3/4-inch slices. Place slices in a 9- by 12-inch baking dish. Pour melted butter over the sliced potatoes. Cover with grated cheese, salt, pepper, and paprika. Bake for 45 minutes or until golden brown.
Yields 4 portions

Special Holiday Whipped Potatoes

8 medium-sized potatoes (peeled)
4 oz. cream cheese
1/4 c. cream (or canned milk)
1/4 c. butter
1/2 tsp. salt
1/8 tsp. pepper
1 egg white lightly beaten

Preheat oven to 350 degrees.
Boil potatoes until soft. Place them in a mixing bowl and add cream cheese, cream (or canned milk), butter, salt, pepper, and last of all the beaten egg white. Mix and put in a greased 9-inch casserole dish and bake for about 35 to 40 minutes or until nicely browned.
Yields 6 to 7 portions

Baked Party Potatoes with Spinach

4 large baking potatoes, baked until almost done
1/2 c. half-and-half cream
1/3 c. butter (or margarine)
1 tsp. salt
2 tsp. sugar
1/4 tsp. black pepper
2 Tbs. finely chopped green onion
1 10-oz. package frozen chopped spinach cooked and well-drained
1 Tbs. chopped parsley
1 Tbs. melted butter

Preheat oven to 375 degrees.
Cut baked potatoes in half. Scoop out baked potato from the skin. Save the shells. Mash the potato with the next six ingredients. Then fold in the cooked and well-drained spinach. Put mixture back into the potato shells, sprinkle with a little chopped parsley and melted butter. Bake for 15 to 20 minutes. This vegetable dish can be prepared ahead and then reheated.
Yields 4 to 8 servings

Sliced Baby Beets

3 c. fresh cooked sliced beets (or canned beets). Reserve juice.
2 Tbs. butter (or margarine)
1 1/2 c. water, including the beet juice
2 Tbs. cornstarch
3 Tbs. sugar
1/4 tsp. salt
1/4 tsp. pepper

In a 2-quart pan melt the butter. In a small bowl mix the water, beet juice, cornstarch, sugar, salt, and pepper. Mix with butter and cook until smooth and thickened. Add the sliced beets and reheat.
Yields 6 to 7 servings

Baked Tomatoes

3 lbs. medium-sized tomatoes
1/2 c. soft butter
1 c. bread crumbs
2 tsp. salt
1 Tbs. Worcestershire sauce

Preheat oven to 400 degrees.
Wash and slice tomatoes in half. Place on baking sheet cut side up. Mix butter, crumbs, salt, and Worcestershire sauce. Place a layer of crumb mixture on each sliced tomato. Bake for 15 to 20 minutes.
Yields 6 to 8 portions

Asparagus Casserole

1 lb. fresh asparagus
1 8-oz. can cream of mushroom soup
1 1/2 c. toasted bread crumbs
1/8 tsp. salt
1/8 tsp. pepper
1 c. Cheddar cheese cut into strips or cubes

Preheat oven to 350 degrees.
Blanch asparagus for 10 minutes in salted, boiling water and drain. Place asparagus in a buttered casserole dish. Add soup, toasted bread crumbs, salt, and pepper. Top with cheese strips. Bake for about 25 minutes.
Yields 5 or 6 servings

Vegetable Cheese Casserole

4 c. diced, peeled potatoes
2 c. diced, peeled carrots
1/2 c. diced small onions
1 c. diced small celery
1/2 c. butter (or margarine)
1/2 c. flour
3 c. milk
3 c. grated Cheddar cheese
1 Tbs. salt
1/2 tsp. pepper
1 box frozen peas
1 c. cracker crumbs

Preheat oven to 350 degrees.
Boil diced potatoes, carrots, onions, and celery for 15 or 20 minutes. Drain. Make a cream sauce with butter, flour, and milk. Add the cheese, stirring until cheese is melted. Season with salt and pepper. Mix peas, cooked vegetables, and sauce. Place mixture in baking dish or individual casseroles and top with cracker crumbs. Bake for 30 to 35 minutes.
Yields 8 to 10 servings

Abbreviations

tsp.	teaspoon
Tbs.	tablespoon
c.	cup
oz.	ounce
pt.	pint
qt.	quart
lb.	pound

Equivalents

1 pinch	1/8 tsp.
3 tsp.	1 tbs.
16 Tbs.	1 cup
1 c. flour	4 oz.
1 c. sugar	7 oz.
1 c. liquid	8 oz.
2 c.	1 pt.
2 pts.	1 qt.
4 qt.	1 gal.
16 oz.	1 lb.
1 lb. water	1 pt. liquid
1 lb. flour	4 c.

Index

Part I

Breads

Pastries

Part II

Soybean Recipes

Part III
Soup

Salads

Finger Foods

Part IV
Entrees

Sauces

Vegetables

ABOUT THE AUTHORS

Jan Willemse is a native of the Netherlands. His training as a cook began at age twelve, in his hometown of Hilversum. Jan eventually went to sea as an apprentice cook, but after several years left the sea life and settled in America. He found employment in Boston, where he met and married his wife Annie. Together they followed the seasonal hotel trade from Maine to Florida. When Edsel Ford beckoned, Jan was hesitant about moving to the "wilderness of Dearborn, Michigan," but within a few years he was persuaded. The result was his introduction to Henry Ford and the soybean. When Henry Ford passed away, so did the Ford enthusiasm for soybean by-products. Jan then left the Ford employ and developed a successful catering business. Jan's final career move was to the Miesel company as a salesman. His knowledge of the preparation of food soon made him one of the company's top salesmen. Eventually Miesel merged with Sysco, and Jan was asked to be the company's Executive Chef, to demonstrate food products, and to represent the wholesaler at food conventions. Jan's association with Henry Ford and the use of the soybean as a food ingredient made him popular and in demand as a speaker. Jan had written several recipe booklets for Miesel/Sysco and with much encouragement decided to publish a cookbook and include the recipes that he had prepared for the Fords. Jan retired from Miesel/Sysco in 1992 at age ninety-two. He now enjoys his garden and still bakes soybean cookies.

Eleanor Eaton, a native of Chicago, moved to Michigan with her widowed mother and brother in the 1930s to attend Hillsdale College and the University of Michigan. After graduating from the University of Michigan she took graduate classes in journalism there. Then she taught music, art, and English in the Hazel Park, Michigan, public schools.

She has lived in Dearborn for forty-seven years, serving as publicity chair on the Board of Directors of the Dearborn Orchestral Society during the orchestra's formative years. Later, she became Women's Editor and columnist of the *Dearborn Times-Herald* newspaper. Since retiring she authored the book, *Dearborn; a Pictorial History*, which was published by Donning Company/Publishers. Currently she is completing a number of fiction and non fiction stories and books. She has three grown children and five grandchildren.